J 917
c.1
Morrison,

Nicaragua /

c2002.   7-03

HA CASS COUNTY PUBLIC LIBRARY
400 E. MECHANIC
HARRISONVILLE, MO 64701

Nicaragua

Nicaragua

by Marion Morrison

Enchantment of the World
Second Series

Children's Press®

A Division of Scholastic Inc.

New York Toronto London Auckland Sydney
Mexico City New Delhi Hong Kong

0 0022 0217936 8

HA CASS COUNTY PUBLIC LIBRARY
400 E. MECHANIC
HARRISONVILLE, MO 64701

Frontispiece: Volcano San Cristobal in the background

Consultant: David Close, Ph.D., Professor, political science, Memorial University of Newfoundland, St. John's, Newfoundland, Canada

Please note: All statistics are as up-to-date as possible at the time of publication.

Book production by Herman Adler Design

Library of Congress Cataloging-in-Publication Data

Morrison, Marion
    Nicaragua / by Marion Morrison.
      p. cm. — (Enchantment of the world. Second series)
    Includes bibliographical references and index.
    ISBN 0-516-20963-9
    1. Nicaragua—Juvenile literature. [1. Nicaragua.] I. Title. II. Series.
  F1523.2 .M67 2002
  972.85—dc21   00-066038

© 2002 by Children's Press®, a Division of Scholastic Inc.
All rights reserved. Published simultaneously in Canada.
Printed in the United States of America.
1 2 3 4 5 6 7 8 9 10 R 11 10 09 08 07 06 05 04 03 02

Acknowledgments

Marion Morrison would like to thank the friendly and open people of Nicaragua who helped with accounts of their lives, the Embassy of the Republic of Nicaragua in London, and the librarians at Canning House, London. Particular thanks to the poets of Solentiname and Katabasis for permission to quote from their work. Also to Gary Willis, Jason Howe, and Peter and Angela Williams for reports on some isolated regions.

Cover photo:
Child pounding maize

Contents

Waterfront homes

A mestizo woman

Land of Poets

NICARAGUA IS AN EXTRAORDINARILY BEAUTIFUL COUNTRY. Sadly, most people know it only as one of those republics in Central America that is featured in the news when devastating earthquakes or hurricanes strike.

Throughout their history, the people of Nicaragua have had to survive disasters of many kinds. Nicaraguans have had to live through dictatorships and revolutions. During the 1960s and 1970s, revolutionaries fought to free their country from the grip of dictators who had been in control for more than forty years. They succeeded in the end, and now Nicaragua has a democratic government.

Natural forces have brought destruction through erupting volcanoes, sudden earthquakes, and sweeping hurricanes. Several towns and villages sit in the shadows of Nicaragua's many volcanoes. Some volcanoes have not stirred for centuries. Others, however, regularly erupt, spewing fire and hot lava.

Nicaragua has also been jarred by unpredictable and frequent earthquakes. Managua,

Opposite: **A carriage rolls past a cathedral in Granada.**

An ice cream vendor pushes his cart past a building.

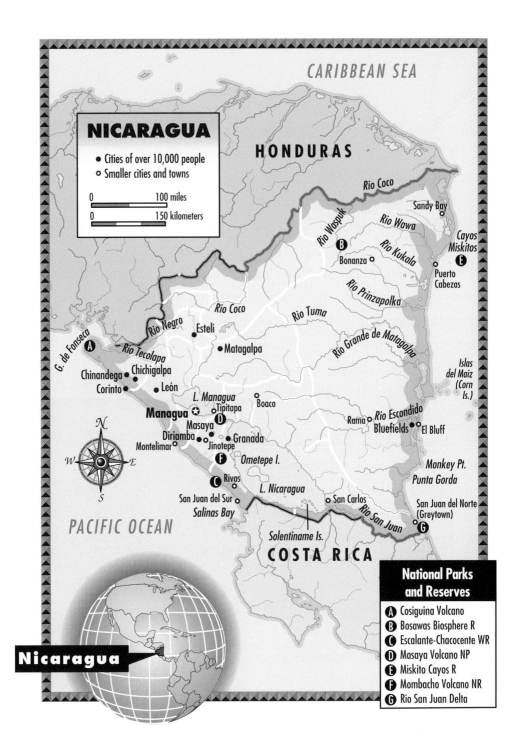

CARIBBEAN SEA

NICARAGUA

- Cities of over 10,000 people
- Smaller cities and towns

| 0 | 100 miles |
| 0 | 150 kilometers |

HONDURAS

Rio Coco

Sandy Bay

Rio Waspuk

Rio Wawa

Cayos
Miskitos

B

Bonanza

Rio Kukala

Puerto
Cabezas

E

Rio Prinzapolka

Rio Coco

Rio Tuma

Esteli

Rio Negro

G. de Fonseca

A

Rio Tecolapa

Matagalpa

Rio Grande de Matagalpa

Islas
del Maiz
(Corn
Is.)

Chinandega

Chichigalpa

Corinto

León

L. Managua

Boaco

Tipitapa

Managua ☆

D

Masaya

Diriamba

Jinotepe

Granada

Montelimar

F

Ometepe I.

Rama

Rio Escondido

Bluefields

El Bluff

Monkey Pt.
Punta Gorda

C

Rivas

L. Nicaragua

San Juan del Sur

Salinas Bay

San Carlos

Rio San Juan

San Juan del Norte
(Greytown)

G

PACIFIC OCEAN

Solentiname Is.

COSTA RICA

Nicaragua

National Parks
and Reserves

- **A** Cosiguina Volcano
- **B** Bosawas Biosphere R
- **C** Escalante-Chacocente WR
- **D** Masaya Volcano NP
- **E** Miskito Cayos R
- **F** Mombacho Volcano NR
- **G** Rio San Juan Delta

Destruction caused by Hurricane Mitch

the capital, was almost completely destroyed in 1972. In addition, the earthquake caused a landslide near San Cristobal, Nicaragua's highest volcano. As mud covered nearby towns, more people died. The earthquake also created floods that swamped the country in many places. More recently, Hurricane Mitch swept through the country taking everything in its path. Villages, towns, bridges, and the country's coffee harvest vanished in a few hours. Many people lost their lives. Yet somehow through all these natural disasters, Nicaraguans continue to make a living from the fertile slopes of the volcanoes, from the oceans, and from the lowlands in the east.

Children in market area of Granada

Nicaragua, the largest country in Central America, has a small but mixed population. People in the western areas are mostly descended from Europeans and Indians, and those in the east are of African and European origin. Mountain ranges separate these groups of Nicaraguans. Getting from one side of the country to the other remains a difficult journey. It is the diverse nature of the people and their fantastic landscape that makes Nicaragua so challenging.

The spectacular, varied environment may also be the route to a more prosperous future. Ecotourism is increasing in Central America, because people want to visit places rich in plant and animal life. At the same time, they do not want to damage the environment. Nicaragua's response has been to create national parks and reserves. Within these different habitats are many fascinating species of animals, including parrots inside an active crater in the Masaya Volcano and freshwater sharks found only in Lake Nicaragua.

A market scene in Puerto Cabezas

Murals often express political subjects.

This monument in Managua honors Rubén Darío.

Despite all the turmoil and tragedies that have taken place in Nicaragua, creativity thrives there. It is expressed through Nicaragua's art and music, but especially through its poetry. It is evident not only in the works of famous poets such as Rubén Darío and Ernesto Cardenal, but also through the efforts of ordinary people—people touched by events.

Some remarkable poems have been written by people of a tiny community near Lake Nicaragua, which reflect much that has happened to them and to their country in recent times. They live in the far southeast of the lake in Solentiname, an archipelago of about thirty islands and islets of pine and balsa trees. The region is isolated. The nearest town

Solentiname archipelago

is the regional capital of San Carlos. It is an hour away by boat across turbulent water, surrounded by lush tropical rainforest.

Their lives were changed with the arrival in 1966 of Father Ernesto Cardenal. He and his colleagues wanted to establish a Catholic community on the islands. Cardenal already had an international reputation as a poet. He soon recognized that the local people had artistic talent and he encouraged them by supplying paints and brushes. When one artist sold a painting in Managua, a flourishing business began. The colorful primitive paintings and artifacts reflecting the islanders' simple way of life became very popular, and sold well both in Nicaragua and abroad. Money was used for education and medical help, and to improve living conditions.

Several of the islanders had a natural, intuitive feel for poetry. As time went on, the paintings began to contain a political message. They were revolutionary and against the dictatorship that was then controlling the country. As Cardenal became more deeply involved in fighting the government, so did many of the young men and women who surrounded him.

In 1976, a poorly trained and ill-equipped group from Solentiname, including a number of poets, attacked a National Guard quarters. One young woman wrote the following poem about the event.

At the Time of the Assault on the San Carlos Barracks
By Olivia Silva and translated by Peter Wright
At nightfall on the twelfth of October
We slip into the Guacalito River.
The monkeys howl as they see us pass.
Palm-trees, and the foul stench of sludge.
Clouds of mosquitoes sting the children's faces.
I am tense and nervous. There is only the crickets' song
And the cry of the weird night-bird seeming to say:
The people will win.

Several poets died in the attack. Others escaped into exile only to die later in the fighting. The government took its revenge by attacking and destroying the community school, library, and church.

The islanders went on writing poems. After the war, the new government helped rebuild the community. Today, the islanders continue their simple lives much as before, selling their paintings and handicraft. But a lifetime of struggle is recorded in their poems read worldwide. Here is an example of their poems.

Wood-carved handicraft in Solentiname

The Red Flame-Tree
by Pedro Pablo Meneses,
translated by Peter Wright
Red flame-tree
Golden trumpet-tree in flower on the island of La Cigueña.
Turtles coming ashore to lay their eggs at full moon.
Night-jars singing.
The plains burnt dry.
Deer drinking along the arid shore.
The first rains have fallen.
There's a smell of damp earth. Flycatchers sing joyfully.
It's May in Solentiname.

Land of Lakes and Volcanoes

Nicaragua straddles the Central American isthmus, from the Caribbean Sea on the Atlantic side to the Pacific Ocean. However, it has a total coastline of only 565 miles (910 kilometers). The republics of Honduras and Costa Rica lie north and south, respectively. Nicaragua is only slightly smaller than the state of Florida and has three distinct regions.

Lowlands bordering the Pacific are fertile and important for agriculture. More lowlands fringe the Caribbean. This eastern coastal part is often known collectively as the

Opposite: **Boys swimming in Lake Nicaragua**

Farming in the lowlands

A mother and her child seek shelter after heavy rains.

Mosquito/Miskito Coast. It has the greatest rainfall in Central America. Between the two lowlands lie the forested central highlands which are deeply dissected by rivers.

Here in sparsely populated *cordilleras*, or mountain chains, are the highest points of Peñas Blancas which reaches 5,725 feet (1,745 meters) in the Cordillera Isabella, and Pico Mogotón at 6,913 feet (2,107 m) in the Cordillera Dipicto y Jalapa on the Honduran frontier.

Perhaps the greatest feature of the country is a shallow basin virtually linking the oceans. The chain of lakes and rivers lies almost diagonally from northwest to southeast. The most extensive of the lakes, Lake Nicaragua is 95 feet (29 m) above sea level, and 100 miles (161 km) long by 45 miles (72 km) wide. It is the largest lake in Central America.

Lake Nicaragua

Lake Nicaragua is the country's dominant physical feature. Its name originated from *cocibolca*, an Indian word that means a

Nicaragua's Geographical Features

Area: 49,998 square miles (129,494 sq km)

Highest Elevation: Pico Mogotón, 6,913 feet (2,107 m) above sea level

Lowest Elevation: Sea level along the Pacific Ocean

Longest River: Rio Coco, 485 miles (780 km)

Largest Lake: Lake Nicaragua, 3,150 square miles (8,159 sq km)

Greatest Annual Precipitation: 297 inches (755 cm), at Bluefields

Lowest Annual Precipitation: 46 inches (117 cm), at Managua

Average Annual Temperature: 80°F (27°C). There is less than 4°F (2.2°C) difference between winter and summer temperatures.

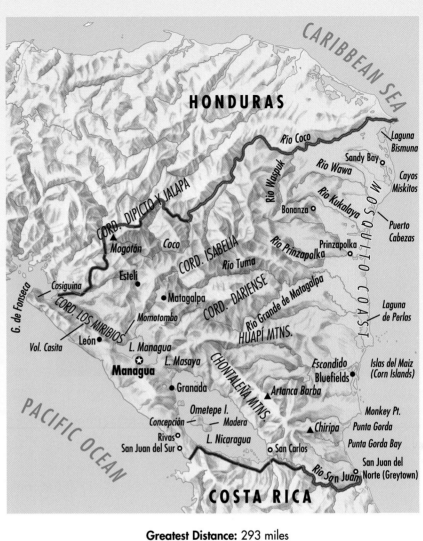

Greatest Distance: 293 miles (472 km), north to south; 297 miles (478 km), east to west

"freshwater sea." The word *Nicaragua* was introduced later by the Spaniards. The origin of the lake stems from earthquakes. The land was raised, perhaps closing a bay of the Pacific coast. More likely it was a rift between faults in the land that filled with fresh water. On the western side, the elevated land

Lake Nicaragua and Volcano Concepción on Ometepe Island

dividing the lake from the ocean is so narrow that in one place, the Rivas Isthmus, near the city of Rivas, is only 12 miles (19 km) across.

Ometepe Island, 16 miles (26 km) long by 8 miles (13 km) wide, is one of about 400 islands scattered around the lake. On it are the twin volcanoes of Concepción and Madera. To the northwest a short river called the Rio Tipitapa connects Lake Nicaragua to Lake Managua where the capital city, Managua, stands on the southern shore.

Volcanoes

Like its Central American neighbors, Nicaragua is on the Ring of Fire girdling the Pacific. A string of volcanoes, some inactive, line the western edge of Nicaragua from the Gulf of Fonseca in the north to Salinas Bay in the south.

The most northerly is Cosiguina, which forms a small peninsula jutting into the Gulf of Fonseca. Cosiguina is not very high at 2,777 feet (847 m) and had not erupted for more than a century when it exploded in 1835. But it did so with such violence that ash reached Mexico City nearly 900 miles (1,448 km) away.

Earthquake!

Earthquakes and volcanic eruptions have punctuated Nicaragua's history. Far beneath the surface of the land, Earth's great crustal plates are always moving. They usually cause no more problems than the rattle of a cup on a saucer or a shudder rumbling through a house.

Around midnight on December 23, 1972, an earthquake rocked Managua. The quake was only 6.3 on the Richter scale—a moderate earthquake. However, Managua's building construction and the ashy volcanic soil under the city could not withstand even a moderate earthquake. By dawn, everything within 2 miles (3 km) of the city's center had been flattened. More than 5,000 people died, and 50,000 lost their homes in one of the worst natural disasters in Nicaragua's history.

The highest volcano is San Cristobal at 5,724 feet (1,745 m) in the Cordillera Los Maribios overlooking the city of León. On several occasions, this volcano has spewed ash to threaten the nearby communities. Others in the same range have had more

The Ring of Fire

Around the edge of the Pacific Ocean stretches a Ring of Fire—a string of active volcanoes. Nicaragua's many volcanoes lie in this vast circle. Earth's crust is made up of several large masses, called plates. Volcanoes, such as San Cristobal, Cerro Negro, and Momotombo exist along the line where these plates meet. Earthquakes are also common along the Ring of Fire.

Lots of Lava

A quiet volcano is not always a dead volcano. Many active volcanoes lie dormant, or sleeping, for hundreds of years, but they can still be dangerous.

Volcano	Last Eruption
El Viejo, San Cristobal	1997
Masaya	1996
Telica	1994
Concepción	1986
Momotombo	1905

View of Concepción from Lake Nicaragua

serious eruptions. Cerro Negro in 1992 left many people homeless, and the 1606 eruption of Momotombo at 4,126 feet (1,258 m) on the southern tip overlooking Lake Managua devasted León.

One of the highest volcanoes is Concepción—5,286 feet (1,611 m)—on the island of Ometepe in Lake Nicaragua. Concepción has erupted at least twenty-four times since 1883. The most recent eruption occurred in 1986 and active *fumaroles*, vents with steam and sulphurous fumes, exist near the summit. La Madera, Concepción's twin on the southern part of the island, is lower at 4,572 feet (1,394 m). La Madera, which has not erupted in the last 10,000 years, is covered by dense rain forest.

Grasslands and distant hills, central highlands

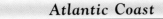

Atlantic Coast

The lowlands on the Atlantic side vary from swamps and broad lagoons to open grasslands and forests. Rain forests are in the northeast near the Coco River and Honduran border. Around Puerto Cabezas are pine savannas that have been shrinking due to nearby construction.

Houses along the Mosquito Coast

The Mosquito/Miskito Coast is difficult to reach by land. Just one good road leads east from Managua to the town of Rama from which boats travel down the Escondido River to the coastal main town of Bluefields.

Offshore are numerous small coral *cayos* or "keys," some with English names. Two small islands, the Big Corn, 6.2 square miles (16 square kilometers), and Little Corn, 1.86 square miles (4.8 sq km), lie east of Bluefields.

Looking at Nicaragua's Cities

León, the second-largest city in Nicaragua, was founded by the Spanish in 1525. It is an important agricultural and business center with a population of about 153,000 people. It is the capital of the department of León and the heart of Nicaragua's northwest farming region. The National University of Nicaragua and two Roman Catholic colleges attract students to the city. A highlight of León is the cathedral, the largest in Central America. Famed Nicaraguan poet Rubén Darío is buried at the cathedral.

At the foot of Mombacho volcano lies the city of Granada, the oldest city in Nicaragua. Granada was first settled in 1523 by the Spanish. The buildings are old, and the city of about 88,000 people is definitely Spanish in style (pictured). Its location on the shores of Lake Nicaragua has provided an interesting history. The area, in the past a lure to pirates and other adventurers, now comprises cattle ranches and haciendas, as well as the factories of major industries. Today, Granada is the commercial center for furniture, soap, clothing, rum, leather, and coffee.

Masaya, a city of about 100,000 people, lies roughly halfway between Lake Nicaragua and Lake Managua. Farmers bring tobacco, coffee, cotton, and cacao to market in Masaya, where those items then flow into the world marketplaces. Visitors to Masaya will find beautiful pottery, clothing, leather goods, and other Nicaraguan handicrafts at the city's open market.

Although much smaller in size, Bluefields is an important port on the Caribbean. Bluefields lies at the mouth of the Escondido River, and is the largest city on the eastern coast. It was settled in 1633 by Abraham

Blauvelt, a Dutch pirate, whose name in English means blue field. Most of Nicaragua bears a Spanish influence. Bluefields, however, is decidedly British. In fact, the region belonged to the United Kingdom until 1860.

A view toward the mountains

Rivers

The rugged core of mountains forming the country's backbone is divided into several *cordilleras* or ranges including Isabella, Dariense, and Chontaleña. Few people live in the highlands. The mountains are the source of rivers that drain eastward to the Miskito Coast or west into the lakes.

In the northern regions the rivers draining toward the Pacific, such as the Negro and Tecolapa (Estero Real), flow into the Gulf of Fonseca, a major inlet shared with Honduras and El Salvador. Rivers on the west are very short, especially those from the narrow ridge of land separating lakes Managua and Nicaragua from the Pacific.

The Rio Grande de Matagalpa as it flows through central Nicaragua

On the eastern side of the central mountains where the rainfall is greater and their courses are longer, rivers have a better chance to develop. Along the Honduran border in the north, the 485-mile (781-km) long Rio Coco empties into the sea. It crosses a broad floodplain dotted with swamps and shallow lagoons.

The Rio Grande de Matagalpa, only 267 miles (430 km) long, drains similarly to a land of lakes and swamps. To the south of this river lies the 37-mile (60-km) long Pearl Lagoon, separated from the Atlantic by a long strip of low-lying land. As its name suggests, this river rises in the Department of Matagalpa on the southern flank of the Cordillera Dariense. A department is similar to a county in the United States, or a province in Canada.

The Rio Escondido, which receives water from several sources including the Rama River in the southern mountains, empties into a shallow bay near Bluefields. In June 2000, the river flooded the small town of Rama, forcing 5,000 people to leave their homes.

The most important river economically is the 124-mile (199-km) long Rio San Juan. Much of this river forms the border with Costa Rica and connects Lake Nicaragua to the sea. These are the waterways that could form the basis of a canal through the isthmus. Except for rapids in three places, shallow draught boats navigate the river for much of its length. It flows mainly through sparsely inhabited country. The Costa Rican side has been developed. However, in Nicaragua the forests and other vegetation are still largely pristine in spite of some settlement by people who were seeking safety from the civil war. The Rio San Juan enters the Caribbean at San Juan del Norte through a delta with major arms in neighboring Costa Rica.

View of Rio San Juan, which carries Lake Nicaragua waters into the Caribbean Sea

Hurricanes put Nicaragua's climate in the news, but most of the time the climate is generally tropical with temperatures ranging from 80 to 95 degrees Fahrenheit (27 to 35 degrees Celsius).

On the western side, there is less rainfall with higher temperatures. The central mountain zone has slightly cooler temperatures according to altitude. On the east, the Atlantic region becomes progressively more humid as the lowlands are reached. A distinct dry season from November to April and a wet season for the rest of the year is normal. Hard rain falls almost all the time on the eastern side of the mountains.

The Department of Carazo

This department lies in the southeast with its border just 29 miles (46 km) from Managua. Carazo department is the third smallest in the country. Only the neighboring departments of Granada and Masaya are smaller.

Much of the land surrounding Carazo is high. The main city, Jinotepe, is a busy commercial center for coffee grown in the surrounding hills where the volcanic soil is among the richest in the country. However, there is high unemployment and people are leaving to find work in Costa Rica. To the west, the land slopes away to fine Pacific coast beaches such as those near the mouth of the Rio Escalente where sea turtles come ashore to lay their eggs.

The hurricane season begins late in the year when storms frequently batter parts of the Caribbean. In recent times, Hurricane Joan will be remembered for flattening Bluefields and Hurricane César for destroying many parts of the Caribbean coast and places inland. Hurricane Mitch created widespread destruction across Central America. At the height of the storm the winds reached 180 miles per hour (290 kph), making it the fourth-strongest on record.

Heavy rains from Hurricane Mitch caused rock avalanches in the northern highlands.

A Wealth
of Wildlife

NICARAGUA'S WIDE-RANGING CLIMATE AND GEOGRAPHY is hospitable to many kinds of plants and animals. With a small population and relatively little disturbance from intensive farming or logging, many natural habitats have remained untouched. Some mangrove forests and lagoons along the Atlantic coast are almost inaccessible. The mountains, especially in the north and east, are often covered with rain forests or dense cloud-soaked forests. These are the largest untouched forests in Central America.

Opposite: **A jaguar, the largest cat in the jungle**

The floor of a cloud forest in northern Nicaragua

National Tree

Nicaragua's national tree is the *madroño*. It grows up to 30 feet (9 m) high, has bell-shaped, white flowers, and belongs to the same plant family as the coffee bush. During the summer, the madroño is covered with blossoms and it stands out among the green of other trees. Its wood is particularly fine-grained and preferred by carpenters and cabinet makers.

Bountiful Forests

The *madroño*, Nicaragua's national tree, is not alone among the great trees of the country. The forests are filled with many that have been used by local people for centuries. The *cedro* or cedar is not of the true cedar family though its reddish wood looks similar. The timber is used in buildings, furniture, and cigar boxes. Its bark can be applied to wounds, which it helps heal by drawing together the tissues. The leaves of the cedro can be added to boiling water and used as a medicine.

Another tree with multiple uses is the balsam, from which medicinal balsam can be extracted. At one time these trees were plentiful around the Gulf of Fonseca in the northwest, though today they have almost disappeared due to their use in rural building. Nicaragua also has pine, oaks, and conifers such as *liquidambar*, another balsam producer.

El Sacuanjoche

The national flower, *el sacuanjoche* or frangipani, grows on a tree that can reach 20 feet (6 m) high. The fragrant blossoms have vivid yellow centers, fading to white on the outside rim of the petals. Perfume invented by an Italian, Sr. Franjipani, is believed to have given the name that the flower is usually called. Occasionally, the blooms are light rose in color, although white and yellow are most common. Outside of Nicaragua, this flower is known as the West Indian jasmine.

The *guayaco* of the drier areas produces a hard wood. It is also well known to the native people of the region for the medicinal properties of its crushed wood. It is now being studied and used in alternative pharmacy.

Plants of the Forest

Even more botanical treasures fill the extensive forests where trees and other plants vary from region to region. Some areas have the broad-leaved evergreen trees of the rain forest. Because the leaves are well adapted to a daily soaking, the water flows away easily from a waxy surface, often cascading from a pointed tip—the "drip tip"—a special feature that has taken tens of thousands of years to evolve.

In these forests, the combination of warmth, humidity, and numerous bacteria and fungi, not to mention the hordes of insects, soon rots the dead vegetation. Epiphytic plants—plants that grow on but are not fed by other plants—are almost universally found on trees, buildings, and even posts carrying wires or on the wires themselves. These plants use the solid base as a support and gather their nutrients in many different ways.

Some of the best known epiphytes are *bromeliads*. Within their whorls of leaves they collect insects, and even small amphibians and reptiles, which decay virtually within the plant. Others, such as the flowing masses of grey beard or Spanish moss, which abound in humid places, collect moisture from the air. They use the tiny hairs on their leaves like pumps that become swollen after rain or in mist and dew.

A three-toed sloth

Forest Life

In the jungles, a background noise of millions of insects is always present and after a while goes unnoticed. Butterflies bring splashes of bright color to the shady places and occasionally migrate across the country in the tens of thousands.

Nicaragua has many unusual animals. Sloths, anteaters, and armadillos are common inhabitants of the forests. Three-toed sloths are slow-moving animals that just inch their way through branches, taking about six hours to cover a mile.

Guardabarrancos

The national bird is the *guardabarranco*, or ravine guard. These multicolored birds are closely related to kingfishers. Guardabarrancos are stunningly beautiful, with brilliant red and yellow feathers and very long green tail feathers. They nest in dry forests or in cleared rain forests where they feed on insects, caterpillars, small lizards, and fruit. They can often be found perched on a branch with their long tail feathers swaying back and forth.

Armadillos feed on a variety of insects and make deep burrows. To see one of these digging is to experience one of nature's best tunneling machines. Nicaragua is home to the

An armadillo

4-foot-long (1-m) Tamandua anteater, which is a good digger armed with tough claws for ripping at termite and ant nests. A smaller, softer, 15-inch (38-cm) two-toed anteater lives in trees where it feeds on termites. As a defense against predators, these tiny anteaters have a prehensile, or actively grasping, tail that can hold a branch with a viselike grip.

The cat family is represented by such species as the puma and the cougar. The jaguar, at up to 300 pounds (136 kilograms), is the largest of them. Others include the jaguarundi or "otter cat," which is smaller, and the margay, marked with a bold pattern of dark brown or black patches. Margays spend much of their lives in the trees hunting for birds in their nests. At night they may venture to the forest floor to hunt for ground-dwelling birds and small mammals, including numerous species of rodents or the rat family.

A puma

Mangroves

Along the Caribbean coast, forests of mangroves are home to waterbirds such as herons and egrets. They are adapted for wading in shallow water where they feed on small fish, mollusks, and insects. On an early morning boat trip through

Mangrove trees

A Wealth of Wildlife **39**

Sharks in Freshwater

The exceptional origin of Lake Nicaragua and the River San Juan has also left some wildlife curiosities. The lake is home to fish such as sharks, tarpon, and sawfish, which are usually encountered in the salty sea. The sharks have been a source of food for generations of lake fishers, though now with increasing demand the fishes' numbers are declining. How they came to be living in a freshwater lake is still being debated.

These fish may have adapted over generations after the lake was sealed off from the ocean. However, that idea now seems unlikely because the lake may never have been part of the Pacific. The freshwater simply flows in from the surrounding mountains. Perhaps the most likely explanation is that the lake-dwellers gradually adjusted to fresh water as they migrated up and down the River San Juan from the Atlantic Ocean.

shallow coastal lagoons one finds herons standing silently, waiting for prey to come within striking distance. A heron uses its bill not to stab, but to grab. Then it swallows and later disgorges pellets of anything it could not digest.

In places around Puerto Cabezas, where the land is sandy, at one time there were many patches of pine savanna or grassland with stands of lowland Caribbean pine. This was the natural vegetation. Today, these pines have been largely destroyed because the wood has been taken as timber. Faring better along the coast are the palm swamps, which are virtually impenetrable and remain natural havens for many birds and small reptiles.

Vampires

Nicaragua struggles with an invasion of vampire bats. Hurricane Mitch destroyed the natural habitat of these blood-drinking bats and forced them to find new homes in Nicaragua's cities and towns.

To attack unsuspecting prey, these bats usually scuttle along the floor ratlike with folded wings. Far from the popular vision of sucking, a vampire bat uses its razor-sharp teeth to make a small cut from which it laps up the oozing blood. Thousands of vampire bats continue to attack people, cattle, and pigs, as local authorities try desperately to control the vampire plague.

Protecting the Wildlife

Nicaraguan authorities have given almost 20 percent of the country the status of Protected Natural Area by developing seventy-five parks or zones. Those on the more accessible Pacific Ocean side are among the best-known sanctuaries.

The beautiful Masaya Volcano National Park was among the first to be established. It is set in a largely dry tropical forest to the north of Lake Masaya. The summit of the Masaya Volcano contains five named craters. It is the most active volcano in the region, and the crater of Santiago emits large quantities of sulfur dioxide gas from a glowing, red-hot interior. Somehow, within this inferno, tiny green parrots known as *chocoyos* have managed to survive. They fly in tight flocks within the crater and nest on rocky ledges.

A flock of parrots at the Masaya Volcano National Park

Another volcano reserve is on Mombacho, which is covered with a fine cloud forest. Here in a perpetually moist environment there is a wealth of epiphytes. Mosses, orchids, and bromeliads abound though settlers pose a threat despite the plants' protected status.

On the Pacific coast, another refuge has been set aside for thousands of sea turtles that emerge from the water at night to lay eggs on the white sand beaches. Lake Nicaragua has a good share of water-birds, ducks, herons, and migrants passing from North to South America and back. In greater isolation, the delta of the River San Juan is another bird watcher's paradise as well as being a home for the manatee or sea-cow, the so-called origin of mermaid stories. Manatees can grow up to 15 feet (5 m) long. They feed by browsing on underwater vegetation. These lumbering beasts breathe in air, but can stay underwater for several minutes. The tiny cayos off the Caribbean shore are havens for migrant birds and turtles.

A sea turtle on the beach

Bosawas Biosphere Reserve

The Bosawas Biosphere Reserve is in an ideal location in northeast Nicaragua. It is difficult to reach because of poor roads, and rarely visited even by ecotourists. Close to the Honduran border, the forests cover mountain ranges to an altitude of 3,281 feet (1,000 m) and include many different ecosystems.

Bosawas covers 14 percent of Nicaragua's land, including the richest surviving forest habitats in Central America. Within the preserve, white-throated capuchin monkeys (pictured) scramble in tall trees and eat fruit, seeds, and even small squirrels. Sloths share trees with them. Deer, jaguars, and ocelots move warily through the forest in search of food.

The reserve is also home to communities of Miskito, descendants of the original Indians, and settlements of mestizo families, or those of mixed Spanish and Indian parents. Both are served by pastors and educators from an evangelical church that also has an interest in the preservation of the environment.

A Challenge

A combination of circumstances has left Nicaragua with a remarkable reservoir of wildlife unique to Central America. The numerous reserves will be costly to manage and even more difficult to keep in isolation. An area such as Bosawas Biosphere Reserve is so large that it is difficult to control what happens inside. As Nicaragua develops, there are threats from loggers and mining operations. The pine forest of the northern central region has already been reduced by settlers. Balsam wood has almost disappeared, and mangroves, especially in the estuaries, are exploited for their wood. Fortunately, the state conservation agency is helped by separate private organizations. Even so, the future for this gem of Central America is uncertain.

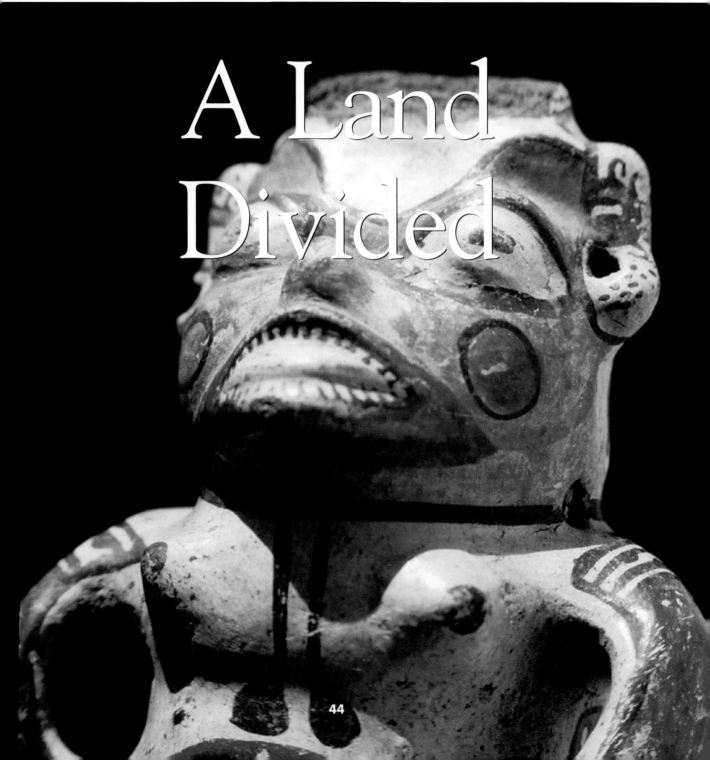

A Land
Divided

44

T HE "FOOTSTEPS OF ACAHUALINCA" ARE THE OLDEST EVI-
dence of humans in Nicaragua. They are preserved in the mud
where they were found on the outskirts of Managua. For thousands of years, the markings had been covered by layers of ash
and volcanic rock. Workers accidentally discovered the fos-
silized footsteps while digging for stone on the edge of an
ancient lake. The footsteps appear to be those of men, women,
children, and some ani-
mals. Experts believe they
died fleeing from a volcanic
eruption, perhaps about
10,000 years ago.

People almost certainly
arrived in the Americas
from Asia tens of thou-
sands of years ago at a time
when it was possible to
cross the frozen Bering
Straits. They survived by
hunting, fishing, and col-
lecting fruits and nuts from
the forests. From about
2000 B.C., they began to
settle, cultivate crops, and
make pottery.

Opposite: **An ancient
terracotta figurine found
on Ometepe Island**

Footsteps of Acahualinca

A painted plate made by ancient Indians living near Lake Nicaragua

Chontales Indians carved this ancient stone statue.

When Spanish explorers arrived early in the sixteenth century, Nicaragua was inhabited by several groups of "Indians." Columbus mistakenly gave this name to the native peoples because he thought he had reached the Indies. The peoples of the central highlands and the Pacific coast are thought to have originated in Mexico. An ancient legend explains that these people were told to travel south until they found a large area of water with two mountains rising from the center. They found the mountains in Lake Nicaragua. They settled there and grew crops such as corn and beans, and raised turkeys and dogs for meat. They drank chocolate on special occasions and also used it as currency—just as the people of Mexico had done. They also spoke dialects of Pipil, a language closely related to Nahuatl, the language of the Aztecs of Mexico.

The major groups in the west were the Nicaindios and the Choroteganos. The Chontal were in the central highlands. Living in separated areas, each tribe had its own chief and nobles. They fought one another, using swords, lances, and arrows made of wood. They also made carvings of jade and other stones, and worked in gold.

The Caribbean lowlands of Nicaragua were inhabited by other tribes. Because of the similarity of their dialects to the Chibchan language spoken in Colombia, they are thought to have migrated north from South America. These tribes were also hunters and fishers who cleared patches of forest to grow cassava (manioc) and plantains. They had little contact with the tribes of western Nicaragua.

The Spanish Conquest

In 1522, the Spanish governor of Panama, Pedro Arias de Avila (known as Pedrarias) sent the explorer Gil González de Ávila to Nicaragua. González received a warm welcome, especially from Nicarao, chief of the Nicaindios tribe. Nicarao agreed to be converted to Christianity along with thousands of his tribesmen.

Later, González met serious resistance from a local chief Diriagén and his army of 3,000 warriors. Diriagén is today a national hero. His counterattack was not strong enough to defeat the Spaniards, but he did force González to return to the coast and to Panama. González and his men left with large quantities of gold and pearls.

A year later, Pedrarias sent another soldier-explorer Francisco Hernández de Córdoba to Nicaragua. Córdoba easily overcame the native peoples. He founded Granada (1523) near Lake Nicaragua and León (1525) near Lake Managua. However, his success made him unpopular with González and Pedrarias, who followed him to Nicaragua. After several months of civil war, Córdoba was arrested and put to death. González died soon after, and Pedrarias stayed in Nicaragua until his own death in 1531.

Hot Chocolate

The chocolate drink native people drank then was nothing like today's sweet, milky hot chocolate. They made a chocolate drink from hot water, unsweetened chocolate, and ground hot red peppers. This burning beverage was believed to give warriors greater strength and stamina.

Naming Nicaragua

Nicaragua took its name from the Nicarao tribe. The tribe's territory lay between Lake Nicaragua and the Pacific Ocean. The Spaniards combined the name, Nicarao, with *agua*, the Spanish word for water.

There was really little in Nicaragua to attract Spanish colonists. They were much more interested in the silver and gold mines of Mexico and South America. Some Spaniards made fortunes by trading Nicaraguan Indians as slaves. Others became farmers and forced the Indians to work for them under the system known as *encomienda*. This meant the Indians had to work for free. In return, they were supposed to receive religious teaching from the landowner. Over the next forty years, the native population of about 1 million decreased to around thirty thousand. Slavery and diseases introduced from Europe were the main reasons for so many deaths.

The colonial years also saw the beginning of a rivalry between the cities of Granada and León that went on until the twentieth century. Granada was associated with the

The Mosquito Coast

The Spaniards had very little to do with the Caribbean lowlands in the east of Nicaragua, though they used the waterway of the Rio San Juan to reach the Atlantic coast. Here their ships became easy targets for pirates and buccaneers, who were mostly British. During the seventeenth century, the British expanded their influence in the region by building trading posts. Timber, sugar, slaves, and the bounty from the Spanish ships were the main commercial enticements.

Three groups of people lived in the wild, densely forested tropical lowlands—the Miskito, the Mayagna, and the Rama. The Miskito were the most powerful because the British gave them guns and ammunition.

They married African slaves whom the British brought from the Caribbean islands. In 1687, a Miskito Chief was crowned "King Jeremy I" by the governor of Jamaica. About fifty years later, the "Kingdom of Mosquitia" became a protectorate of the British Crown.

Before long, the Spaniards grew tired of the continual attacks on their trading ships. They assumed official control over the region. But the Miskito refused to recognize Spanish control, and their power diminished as more Afro-Caribbeans from the West Indies arrived and marriages were made between settlers and African slaves. After Nicaragua became independent, Great Britain again controlled the area, but left finally in 1860.

Early scene of Granada

wealthy upper-class merchants. León, on the other hand, was relatively poor, and home to the middle classes.

Independence

By the beginning of the nineteenth century, most Latin American colonies resented the strong hold Spain had over their administration and trade. They wanted independence. Events in Europe started the ball rolling, when the Spanish king was deposed by French forces in 1808. In 1811, revolu-

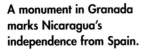

A monument in Granada marks Nicaragua's independence from Spain.

tionaries removed the governor of Nicaragua. The city of Granada supported the revolutionaries, but the city of León remained loyal to Spain. On September 15, 1821, the province of Nicaragua declared its independence from Spain.

In 1822, Nicaragua joined the Mexican Empire, but this lasted only a year. Then, Nicaragua joined with Costa Rica, El Salvador, Guatemala, and Honduras to become part of a Central American Federation. This organization failed because some countries wanted to govern themselves, while others wanted one central government. Nicaragua finally became an independent republic in 1838.

Passage Across the Isthmus

Until the mid-nineteenth century, the United States had little interest in Nicaragua. The turning point came with the Californian gold rush. People and mining equipment needed to be transported across the continent from east to west as quickly as possible. The route from the Atlantic port of San Juan del Norte (then known as Greytown), along the San Juan River to Lake Nicaragua, and then overland to San Juan del Sur on the Pacific coast seemed to offer the best opportunity.

European Exploration & Proposed Canal

—— Columbus, 1502–1504

—— Cortés, 1524

Proposed canal and route by mid-nineteenth century travelers to California

In 1849, the Nicaraguans gave the United States the exclusive right to develop the route. A company belonging to Commodore Cornelius Vanderbilt was to build a canal within twelve years. In return, the United States promised to protect Nicaragua from foreign, namely British, invasion.

The British were far from happy with this arrangement and tried to stop the operations. The United States and Great Britain then agreed to work together, though they did not mention this to the Nicaraguan government. But the disputes continued. The Nicaraguan government also had other problems. One problem was William Walker, an adventurer. Another problem was a civil war. The route was built, but after only five years in use, the route was closed from 1857 until 1862 and completely abandoned in 1868.

Cornelius Vanderbilt

William Walker

The dictionary describes a *filibuster* as a "lawless adventurer or one who engages in unauthorized and irregular war against foreign states." In the nineteenth century, William Walker was the most famous filibuster in Central America.

Walker was born in 1824 in Nashville, Tennessee. After becoming a doctor, he worked as a lawyer and newspaper editor in New Orleans, then moved to California.  Walker was a strong advocate of slavery, and he wanted to create a republic. He seized land in southern California and declared it a separate nation with himself as president. Walker's rebellion was quickly put down and he stood trial. He was acquitted by a jury. Despite his failure, he had gained a reputation as a daring soldier of fortune.

In 1855, Walker and a band of about fifty men went to Nicaragua. He easily took control and set up his own government the following year.

Walker declared himself president of Nicaragua. An ancient Indian legend said that a saviour would come to the Nicaraguan region with light eyes, and Walker often referred to himself as "the grey-eyed man of Destiny." However, once in power he ruled like a tyrant. He angered the Nicaraguans by making English the official language and selling native land to American companies. His support of slavery met with some approval in the United States, but many people in Central America were far from happy.

Walker dreamed of establishing an empire of Central American countries. He wanted to use the canal across the isthmus to attract shipping interests to Central America. He also planned to use slave labor on plantations in the region. Walker's biggest mistakes were underestimating Great Britain's interests in Central America and angering Cornelius Vanderbilt.

Led by Costa Rica, backed by Great Britain, and funded by Cornelius Vanderbilt, the Central American nations declared war. During the "National War," the filibusters were defeated in the battle of Rivas near the Costa Rican border. Walker fled to the United States. Later, he made other attempts to return to Central America, the last in 1860. The British Navy caught him as he tried to enter Honduras. After being turned over to the authorities, he was executed in Trujillo, Honduras. He was only thirty-six years old.

"The Thirty Years"

Compared with the 1840s and 1850s, when Nicaragua had more than thirteen leaders, the last part of the nineteenth century was a period of stability and prosperity. Nicaraguans refer to this period as the Thirty Years.

Several conservative governments were in charge during this period. The exporting of coffee, much in demand in Europe, led to an economic boom. Coffee growers became wealthy and the gap between them and the peasant farmers became wider. But with the profits from coffee and other crops, such as bananas, the government was able to improve communications with new telegraph lines, roads, and railroads.

Another important development occurred in 1857. Granada and León agreed to make Managua the seat of government and effectively the country's capital city.

José Santos Zelaya

Send In the Marines

In 1893, the Liberals, led by José Santos Zelaya, took control in a coup. A coup is when a particular group suddenly takes over a government, often by force. During his sixteen years in office, Zelaya made many improvements. He opened the country to foreign investment, increased coffee and banana production, created a professional army, and built new roads, railroad lines, schools, and government buildings. It was also during his time in office that Mosquitia was officially incorporated into Nicaragua.

Because Zelaya was a dictator, he upset the United States. By the turn of the century, U.S. companies controlled most of Nicaragua's production of coffee, bananas, gold, and timber.

Benjamin Zelaydón

The United States was again interested in constructing a trans-isthmus canal. But Zelaya would not give his permission. His anti-American stance angered conservative groups in Nicaragua who were mostly landowners. In 1909, a revolt broke out. When two U.S. citizens, who had taken part in the revolt were killed, the United States sent 400 marines to Bluefields on the Atlantic coast to support the Conservatives. Zelaya was forced to resign.

But the troubles did not end there. The Liberals and Conservatives continued to be at each other's throats. In 1912, the United States was again asked to send in marines when a Liberal force led by Benjamin Zelaydón threatened to unseat the Conservative government. When Zelaydón's revolt crumbled, he was killed. U.S. marines remained in Nicaragua until 1933.

During this time, Nicaragua signed various treaties which gave the United States more control over Nicaraguan affairs. In 1916, the two countries agreed to the Chamorro-Bryan Treaty. This treaty gave the United States the rights to build a canal across Nicaragua.

In 1925, believing the Conservatives to be well-established in government, the United States withdrew the marines. But the next year the marines returned to stop a Liberal revolt. In 1927, most of the rival parties agreed to put down their arms and work together democratically. They signed the Pact of Espino Negro. One rebel leader, however, would not sign. He was Augusto César Sandino.

U.S. marines in Nicaragua

Augusto Sandino

Augusto Sandino was born in 1895. As a young man he spent time in Honduras, Guatemala, and Mexico. During his travels, he was influenced by the new ideas of communism and support for indigenous peoples. Returning to Nicaragua in 1926, he found work in a U.S.-owned gold mine and was soon lecturing the workers on social injustice.

Sandino formed a small army of workers and peasants. He vowed to wage his guerrilla campaign until the last U.S. marine had left the country. The marines left in 1933. However, in 1934, while in the middle of negotiations with the government, Sandino was arrested and executed by the National Guard.

Sandino, leading his Army for the Defense of Nicaraguan Sovereignty, continued to fight. But by the 1930s, the United States was tiring of the guerrilla war, and upset by the growing list of casualties. A plan was devised so that U.S. troops could go home. It was agreed that the North Americans would train a Nicaraguan National Guard to take over their job. Although Sandino had agreed that he would stop fighting once the marines left, he changed his mind because he believed the National Guard was a tool of the U.S. government.

As a compromise, President Sacasa offered Sandino and his men an amnesty. One night, after dinner with the president, Sandino was murdered. The person behind the assassination was the head of the National Guard, Anastasio "Tacho" Somoza Garcia. He was a very ambitious man who feared Sandino might persuade the president to get rid of the National Guard. With Sandino out of the way, Somoza Garcia was on the first step of a ruthless road to power. Once Somoza Garcia gained control of the country, he and his sons controlled Nicaragua for forty-two years.

The Somozas

Anastasio Somoza Garcia became president in 1937. He retained his position as head of the National Guard and used it to control virtually everything in Nicaragua from the radio stations to the public health service. He appointed only friends and relatives to important government and legal jobs. He bribed supporters to keep them loyal. Within a year, he was in a strong enough position to declare that he would stay in power beyond his presidential term.

Somoza Garcia was educated in the United States and understood North American culture. He knew he had to remain friendly with the U.S. government. To convince the United States, he created a government that was similar to a democratic government. He found ways to stay in power without appearing to override the constitution. The National Guard dealt with any opposition.

During World War II, it suited Somoza Garcia to declare Nicaragua's support for the Allies and the United States. Already enormously wealthy from coffee and cattle ranching, his fortunes soared with increased exports of timber, gold, and cotton. His family owned most of these industries. By the end of the war, the president was one of the richest men in Central America.

This was a turning point. The majority of Nicaraguans were still very poor, and the Somozas' wealth made them very angry. By this time, the United States no longer trusted Somoza Garcia. In 1944, Somoza Garcia's opponents felt confident enough to protest openly in massive demonstrations. Once again he deceived them. He placed another person as the new president, and made various promises to the labor unions. By also making peace with the United States, he managed to stay in power. However, in September 1956, he was assassinated by a young poet.

He was succeeded by his sons. The elder, Luis, became president, and Anastasio "Tachito" took over as head of

Anastasio Samoza Garcia (center) and his sons, Luis Somoza Debayle and Anastasio Somoza Debayle

the National Guard. Luis seemed not as ruthless as his father. But Anastasio preferred brute force. Together, they rigged the elections and appointed friends to important positions. They also impressed the United States by being strongly anti-communist, even supplying bases on the Caribbean coast for the Bay of Pigs invasion in Cuba in 1961.

End of the Somozas

In 1967, Anastasio Somoza Debayle became president. It took the 1972 earthquake to reveal just how corrupt his regime was.

The Sandinistas

In 1961, a group of university students led by Carlos Fonseca, Silvio Mayorga, and Tomás Borge (pictured) formed the Sandinista National Liberation Front (FSLN—Frente Sandinista de Liberación Nacional), named after Augusto Sandino. The Sandinistas began as followers of Karl Marx, a German who believed that wealth should be spread evenly among all the people of a country. Marx's theory is the basis for Communism.

The Sandinistas' aim was to overthrow the Somozas. Many young people, inspired by Fidel Castro and the Cuban revolution two years earlier, volunteered to join. As a small, ill-equipped group they were not able to make much headway during the 1960s. Occasionally, though, some successes against the National Guard gave them good publicity.

The Sandinistas continued to fight through the 1970s. In 1979, they forced the last Somoza into exile. That year, the political branch of the Sandinistas came to power. The Sandinistas remained in government for eleven years.

After the earthquake, members of the National Guard were involved in the widespread looting of homes and businesses. They also took food that overseas organizations had sent to help victims of the earthquake and sold it to people on the streets. Money intended for earthquake victims also found its way into Somoza government accounts. Anastasio Somoza Debayle later denied these things, but few believed him. By 1974, the president's personal wealth was estimated at US$400 million. People in Nicaragua and in other countries were angered.

As the opposition mounted, so did the confidence of the newly formed Sandinista movement, the FSLN. In 1974, the Sandinistas kidnapped several Nicaraguan officials, including Somoza family members. The FSLN demanded and received a ransom of $1 million and the release of fourteen prisoners.

Chamorro (right) was editor of *La Prensa.*

The Somoza government became even more repressive. In 1974, Anastasio Somoza Debayle was again "re-elected" president. By now opposition politicians, wealthy businessmen, the Church, and the Sandinistas were working together. President Jimmy Carter threatened to cut off military aid to Nicaragua unless human rights improved.

Pedro Joaquín Chamorro Cardenal, leader of the opposition and editor of a major newspaper, *La Prensa*, was assassinated in January 1978. A nationwide strike and mass demonstrations followed. The

National Guard still remained in control, but their ruthless tactics led the United States to stop military aid to Nicaragua.

In 1978, the FSLN stormed the National Palace and took 2,000 people hostage—government workers and legislators alike. President Somoza gave way to their demands. Nevertheless, the following year, Somoza announced that he would extend his term in office to 1981. But this time, the opposition and FSLN had the upper hand. By the middle of 1979, the Sandinistas had control of most of the country. They forced Somoza to resign and flee to Miami, Florida. A year later, he was assassinated in Paraguay.

Daniel Ortega

Revolutionaries in Power

The FSLN created a new government, the Junta of National Reconstruction (JNR). It included the Sandinista Daniel José Ortega Saavedra and Violeta Barrios de Chamorro, widow of the assassinated Pedro Chamorro.

The country faced enormous problems. At least 50,000 people had been killed, and more than half a million had been made homeless. About 120,000 people had fled into exile, many of them skilled professional people. The economy was in ruins, and few people had land that they could farm. The majority of people were very poor, food was scarce, and medical help almost nonexistent. The country owed millions of dollars to international banks and organizations.

The U.S. Congress approved an aid package of millions of dollars. The Sandinistas took over the banks and businesses. They also took over the Somoza properties, which added up to more than 20 percent of Nicaragua's best land. The government organized a literacy campaign, and made great improvements in health care.

Not everyone approved of the government's program. Violeta de Chamorro thought it had gone too far. Others felt it had not gone far enough and split from the main party. *Campesinos*, people from rural areas, were frustrated by the long delays in carrying out land reforms. In the Mosquitia region, people were hostile to the FSLN's clumsy attempts to relocate them from their traditional homes.

Chief among the opposition to the FSLN were former National Guard members, many of them exiled in Honduras. The United States also worried about Nicaraguan links with the Soviet Union and Cuba. When President Ronald Reagan took office in 1980, he suspended aid to Nicaragua. In 1982, he authorized millions of dollars for recruiting and training Nicaraguan counter-revolutionaries, called *Contras*. By the mid-1980s about 15,000 Contras were training in Honduras and Costa Rica. In response, the Sandinistas required all men over age sixteen to join the army. The government had to use

Contras in training

money to pay for the war, which should have been spent on the social needs of the people.

In 1985, the U.S. Congress voted to stop funding the Contras. President Reagan then announced a trade embargo preventing U.S. companies from doing business with Nicaragua. Until that time, the United States had been Nicaragua's main trading partner. The embargo, combined with the on-going war, had a devastating effect on the Nicaraguan economy. As the situation deteriorated, the Sandinistas themselves resorted to repressive measures, human rights violations, and press censorship.

Meanwhile, in the United States, the Irangate scandal was unfolding. Although Congress had decided not to back the counterrevolutionaries, members of the Reagan government

The Chamorros

When the Chamorros first arrived in Nicaragua from Spain in the eighteenth century, they settled in Granada. During the nineteenth century, two family members became president. The most prominent Chamorro was Emiliano Chamorro Vargas (1871–1966). Known as the Lion of Nicaragua, he served as president from 1917–1921. He was active in politics all his life, but when he failed to win the presidency a second time, he went into exile.

The great grand-nephew, Pedro Chamorro, who was the leader of the opposition and editor of *La Prensa*, was assassinated in 1978. His wife, Violeta, took over the management of the newspaper and continued her late husband's opposition activities. She was elected president in 1990. But the Sandinista revolution split the family. Violetta had become disillusioned with the Sandinista government, thinking its politics too radical. Her newspaper reflected her ideas and was shut down by the Sandinistas in 1986. At the time of her election, Violeta Chamorro's eldest son and youngest daughter worked on *La Prensa* which had reopened. But her eldest daughter was a Sandinista diplomat, and her youngest son was editing the Sandinista daily newspaper, *Barricada*. Pedro's own brothers and a number of cousins in prominent positions also had opposing political views. It remains to be seen which Chamorro will hit the political headlines next.

were selling arms to Iran and sending the money to the Contras. The U.S. Central Intelligence Agency also was involved in helping the Contras.

By 1987, all sides were prepared to enter peace talks. An agreement was reached and the Sandinistas promised national elections in 1990. The elections went ahead, with a result that astonished almost everybody.

A New Direction

In the 1990 election, Violeta Chamorro, leader of the coalition, anti-Sandinista UNO (the United National Opposition) defeated Daniel Ortega. The Sandinistas, and the world at large, were stunned. They had been confident of winning the election.

The United States supported the UNO. After the election the United States called off the trade embargo and cut off sup-

Violeta Chamorro celebrates her victory.

Arnoldo Alemán

plies to the Contras. Fearing further violence between the Sandinistas and Contras, Chamorro agreed that Sandinista officers could keep their positions in the army. Ortega's brother continued as head of the military. The Contras were invited to return to Nicaragua from Honduras, provided they turned in their weapons. Many followed orders, but others chose to fight on. These rebels became known as *recontras*.

Chamorro completed her six years in office, though many people believed that her son-in-law, Antonio Lacayo, was in control. Peace finally came to Nicaragua and the economy improved, but divisions within the UNO had surfaced, with right-wing support going to the Liberal Constitutionalist Party (PLC). The party was led by an ex-mayor of Managua, Arnoldo Alemán. In 1996, he was elected president.

Alemán's Government

The inauguration of Arnoldo Alemán in 1997 marked only the second transfer of power in Nicaragua's recent history of one democratically elected president to another. He was supported by wealthy people, the Catholic Church, and many poor people of Managua who had witnessed the U.S.-style developments he had introduced when he was mayor. Though the poor people could not afford the drive-in movies, fast-food restaurants, or shopping malls, they approved of the changes.

Alemán had made a number of campaign promises, including improving the economy and settling the land problem. He has achieved some of his objectives. However, the economy remains weak, and poverty is still widespread. His government has been accused of corruption. Recently, workers and students have carried out demonstrations and strikes against the government.

The relationship between Nicaragua and the United States has improved in recent years, especially after U.S. troops helped after the destruction caused by Hurricane Mitch. Now the two governments are cooperating in the drug war, a problem in the whole Central American region.

There has been tension between Nicaragua, Honduras, and El Salvador over a territorial dispute in the Caribbean waters of the Gulf of Fonseca. In early 2000, armed clashes occurred between Honduras and Nicaragua. The case has been taken to the International Court of Justice in the Hague.

Sandinista Split

Following his defeat to Violeta Chamorro, Daniel Ortega's position as leader of the FSLN was challenged. Some members of the party thought he had too much power. A former vice-president of the FSLN, Sergio Ramirez, called for democratic reform. Sandinistas began to take sides. In September 1994 Ramirez resigned. In the next year, he formed the Sandinista Renovation Movement (MRS). Many professional people joined his party, including two-thirds of the FSLN representatives in the National Assembly. However, in the 1996 election the MRS gained just one seat in the Assembly compared with the FSLN's thirty-five seats.

Governing Nicaragua

THE SANDINISTA GOVERNMENT OF NATIONAL RECONSTRUCtion introduced a new Constitution in January 1987. According to the Constitution, the executive branch is directed by a president. The president is head of state, head of government, and commander-in-chief of the defense and security forces of the nation. The Constitution states that the president should be elected every six years. Violeta Chomorro's government amended the term of office to five years. Neither the president nor a close relative can be re-elected for a second consecutive term.

The president is assisted by a vice president who appoints abinet of ministers. The ministers have various responsibilies including foreign affairs, finance, agriculture, defense, transport, education, and health. The president also appoints the head of the Central Bank and ambassadors who represent Nicaragua in other countries.

Opposite: **Government building in Managua**

The National Flag

Nicaragua's flag has three equal horizontal bands of blue, white, and blue. Blue stands for justice and loyalty. White represents purity and integrity. The Nicaraguan coat of arms is displayed at the flag's center. The seal is a triangle signifying equality. A rainbow inside the triangle represents peace. Five volcanoes express unity and brotherhood with other Central American countries. The flag was adopted in 1908.

Meeting of the National Assembly

Legislative and Judicial Branches

The legislature is the National Assembly. It is made up of ninety elected members who hold office for five years. Defeated presidential candidates may also have a seat in the National Assembly, provided they receive a particular number of votes. At present there are ninety-three members in the Assembly. All citizens over sixteen-years-old have the right to vote.

Since 1995 the power of the National Assembly has greatly expanded. It passes laws, approves the national budget, confirms the appointment of judges to the Supreme Court of Justice, and has the power to override the president under particular circumstances. It also appoints magistrates to the Supreme Electoral Council, a co-equal branch of government responsible for organizing and conducting elections.

NATIONAL GOVERNMENT OF NICARAGUA

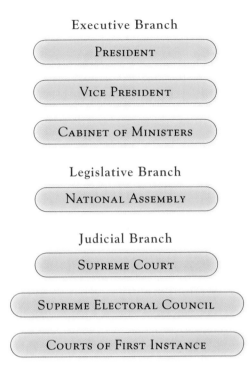

Executive Branch
- President
- Vice President
- Cabinet of Ministers

Legislative Branch
- National Assembly

Judicial Branch
- Supreme Court
- Supreme Electoral Council
- Courts of First Instance

The Supreme Court is the highest court in Nicaragua. It consists of twelve judges nominated by the president and approved by the National Assembly. These judges serve for a term of six years. The court deals with both criminal and civil cases. It also selects the judges for all lower courts. Lower courts, known as the Courts of First Instance, are located in the major cities.

Local Government

Nicaragua has fifteen departments and two autonomous regions on the Caribbean coast, RAAN (Región Autonomo

Atlantica Norte) and RAAS (Región Autonomo Atlantica Sur). Each has a capital city, which often has the same name as the department. For example, León is the capital of the Department of León, and Boaca is the capital of the Department of Boaca. Each capital city has an elected mayor.

Since 1990, Nicaraguans have elected local government officials. Previously they were appointed by the central government. Mayors and vice-mayors for the country's 145 municipalities are elected by secret ballot every four years. RAAN and RAAS have an elected regional council.

Political Parties

From the time of independence until the 1970s, the Liberal and Conservative parties dominated Nicaraguan politics. After the overthrow of the Somozas in 1979, the number of political parties increased. In 1996, thirty-two parties took part in the election. Following government legislation, there are four principal parties.

The Liberal Party gets much of its support from the business community. Their policies include privatizing industry and they welcome foreign investment. Traditionally, the city of León supports the Liberals.

The Sandinistas continue to get support from poor people living in cities and towns, and from organized labor. They want to continue the work they started after the revolution, improving living and working conditions. Medical care, education, and land ownership are particularly important. They want an independent foreign policy rather than being tied to the United States.

Ortega and the Sandinistas

For a long time, Daniel Ortega was the undisputed leader of the FSLN. His father was an ardent opponent of Somoza Garcia, and Daniel was first arrested as a teenager for throwing stones at the U.S. embassy in Managua. He was jailed in 1961 and 1963. Later, he enrolled at the University of Central America to study law, but left after three months to join the newly formed Sandinista group.

Coming from a humble background, he related easily to ordinary people. Hundreds would flock to his meetings, where he rallied them to the Sandinista cause.

During the 1980s when Ortega was able to achieve some of these goals, his popularity was at a peak. Many people were upset when he lost the 1990 election. There is no doubt that the Sandinista Party was damaged by losing the elections in 1990 and 1996, and by splits within the party. Ortega has tried to change his image and was the FSLN presidential candidate in the 2001 election.

The Conservatives have traditionally received support from the city of Granada. They have always been associated with wealthy people, landowners, rural people, and the Church. Today, they are deeply divided and are not a major political force.

The newly formed Christian Path Party came in third in the 1996 elections, though with only 4 percent of the vote. Their campaign is based on faith in God and honesty in government. They are supported by evangelical groups.

In 2000, a clause was added to the Constitution stating that only parties that receive at least 4 percent of the national vote can have seats in the National Assembly. Some people opposed this clause because they felt it would make the 2001 election a race only between the Liberals and the Sandinistas.

Elections and Political Parties

Many people regard 1985 as the first time Nicaraguans had a reasonably fair and democratic election. Today, Nicaraguans

Nicaraguans voting

make the most of their right to vote, and they love to talk about politics. In their houses, at the office, in the marketplace, on buses, in coffee shops, groups of people argue and debate the policies of the day.

Many people joined the Sandinista party; in 1996 it had about 300,000 members. No other new party—and there have been many very small ones—have attracted people in such numbers. Apart from the Sandinistas and those people still loyal to the traditional Liberal and Conservative parties, relatively few Nicaraguans actually belong to a political party.

The National Anthem

The national anthem, called "Nicaragua," was composed in 1918 by the poet Salomon Ibarra Mayorga. It was later revised by musician Luis A. Delgadillo so that the song could be sung by children. The song is considered one of the most beautiful of all national anthems, probably because the lyrics stress the importance of peace.

Nicaraguans respect their national anthem. They stand when they hear it and remove their hats. The anthem is sung at school every Monday morning before classes. It is also sung in businesses on Friday afternoons. The anthem is played at sporting events, political events, and on national holidays.

Managua: Did You Know This?

Managua became the national capital in 1857. The city is also known as *Novia del Xolotolón* (Bride of Xolotlan, a volcano). The population is about 1,295,000—one in four Nicaraguans live in Managua. Most residents of Managua are Roman Catholics. The people of Managua celebrate two saints' days—the Fiesta de Santiago on July 25, and the Fiesta de Santo Domingo on August 1. These holidays feature parades, dancing, and music.

The *Palacio Nacional de la Cultura* is a historic and cultural landmark in Managua. The Cathedral of Santiago is the central church in the city. It is found near the *Palacio Nacional*. Managua also has a campus of the National University.

The city is located on the southern shore of Lake Managua. Two major earthquakes, one in 1931 and another in 1972, struck Managua and destroyed much of the city. The rebuilt city is about 6 miles (9 km) from the original city center. The Pan American Highway runs past Managua and is the main transportation route from the city.

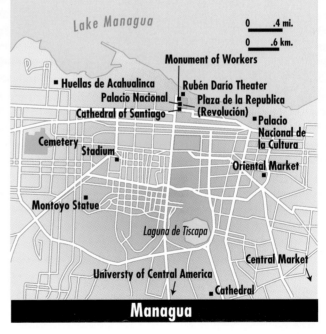

Reviving the Economy

WHEN VIOLETA CHAMORRO CAME TO POWER IN 1990, Nicaragua's economy was bleak. The combined effects of the 1972 earthquake, the 1988 hurricane, a decade of Sandinista government, the Contra War, and years of a U.S. trade embargo had left the country in ruins. The economy was in bad shape despite the fact that Nicaragua had received over a billion dollars in aid from Communist countries since the early 1980s.

Nicaragua's economy has always been based on farming. However, by the 1990s, production of its two main crops, coffee and cotton, had declined. There was virtually no man-ufacturing in the country, and no mining was being carried

Opposite: **Harvesting pitaya fruit**

In the 1980s, this woman works in a factory producing baseballs—the only factory in Nicaragua then.

Destruction caused by Hurricane Joan in 1988

out. Roads, bridges, railroads, and telegraph lines had all been damaged by the war and hurricanes. Guerrillas were blowing up power stations causing electrical blackouts. Oil imports, needed to generate electricity, were very expensive. Exports were down by 40 percent. About half of the people were unemployed.

A New Start

Faced with the challenge of reviving the economy, Chamorro had to adopt a plan acceptable to the World Bank and others to whom Nicaragua owed money. Before they would consider more loans, the international banks made the government reduce spending. This affected education, health, and transportation, all important to workers and to poor people. There were demonstrations and strikes. Between 1990 and 1995 Nicaragua was promised more than $3.2 billion from foreign governments and international financial organizations. The United States also lifted its embargo.

Teachers on strike
in Managua

The Chamorro government introduced a free market and allowed private ownership of many of banks, farms, and companies. This increased the level of unemployment. Many people lost their jobs. In 1992, unemployment reached 60 percent. Workers were persuaded to start small businesses. This resolved the immediate crisis, but led to an increase in the number of "underemployed" for example, people who took part-time jobs or set themselves up as street vendors.

A street vendor

Nicaragua's Currency

Nicaragua's currency is named after the explorer Francisco Hernandez de Córdoba, the Spanish conquistador who founded León and Granada. For many years, córdobas were tied to the value of the U.S. dollar. By 1991, the exchange rate was US$1 = C$6 million. A new currency, the *córdoba oro*, was introduced in 1991 to coincide with new economic policies. It began equal to the dollar, but as a result of inflation and devaluation it now stands at C$13.3 to the dollar. The córdoba is printed in the following note demominations: CS$100, 50, 20, 10, 5, and 1. One córdoba equals 100 centavos. Coin denominations are 50, 25, 10, and 5 centavos.

By 1996, inflation was under control and Nicaragua had the fastest growth rate in Central America. It was also receiving more aid than almost any other country in the world. Poor people in Nicaragua, however, hardly benefited from this wealth, most of which remained in the hands of just 20 percent of the population.

Agriculture (2000 est.)

Sugarcane	4,000,000 metric tons
Corn (maize)	363,636 metric tons
Rice	285,315 metric tons
Bananas	91,636 metric tons
Coffee	81,818 metric tons

Manufacturing (1995; *in cordobas*)

Food, beverages, tobacco	$C3,129,000,000
Machinery, metal products	$C319,000,000
Refined petroleum, rubber products	$C231,000,000

Mining (1993)

Gold	42,300 troy ounces

A worker picks coffee berries

Coffee and Crops

Agriculture, which includes forestry, fishing, and live-stock, accounts for about two-thirds of the money Nicaragua earns from its exports. More than 40 percent of the people work in agriculture. Many who live in rural areas work on large farms or grow their own food on small plots of land.

The most important crop is coffee. It was first grown as a curiosity in the early 1800s. Commercial cultivation began in the area around Managua in the 1840s. Later, large areas of western Nicaragua were also turned over to coffee plantations.

Coffee provides thousands of men, women, and children with seasonal work. During the harvest from

November to January, they make their way from all parts of the country to the north where the mountain slopes are covered in rows of dark-green coffee bushes. Workers collect the ripened red berries in baskets. They are paid according to the weight they pick, but seldom make more than a few dollars a day. The money they earn is often what they live on for the rest of the year.

Coffee is Nicaragua's main export. As with many crops, coffee production is based on the weather. Hurricanes and floods can wipe out a year's harvest within hours. The value of the export crop is also affected by

Sacks of coffee being exported from Nicaragua

competition from other countries. If the coffee price falls too low, it can spell disaster for countries such as Nicaragua that rely basically on one major export crop.

Picking cotton

Nicaragua's other export crops include sugarcane, bananas, and cotton. Cotton was an important industry until it collapsed from international competition and low world prices in the 1980s. The banana industry also faces strong competition from other countries. The sugar industry was badly disrupted by the U.S. embargo in the 1980s. The United States had been Nicaragua's main export market.

The most important food crops are rice, maize, and beans. Nicaragua imports both rice and wheat. Many small farmers

Shrimp fishing on the
Caribbean coast

can no longer afford tools, seeds, and fertilizers, nor can they easily borrow money from the banks.

Foreign investment has helped to create some new agricultural industries. These include seafood, particularly shellfish, melons, and onions.

Expanding Industry

Nicaragua has a variety of mineral resources, including deposits of gold, silver, copper, lead, antimony, zinc, and iron. Manufacturing employs about 13 percent of the population. People work in factories, producing processed food and drink, petroleum by-products, and

Resources

Cereals	C Copper	S Silver
Tropical crops	G Gold	Z Zinc
Forests	L Lead	
Swamps		

A man makes jeans in a Free Trade Zone factory.

chemicals. Relatively new in Nicaragua, but well established elsewhere in Central America, is a Free Trade Zone where foreign-owned *maquila* factories are exempt from certain protective laws. These factories produce clothing, footwear, and jewelry. The work, however, is tedious, the hours long, the pay low, and the warehouse-like conditions often cramped as row upon row of machinists turn out pre-cut garments or stitch shoes.

Tourists Are Welcome

Tourism has become an important source of income—more people are visiting Nicaragua than ever before. In January 2000, the first cruise ship arrived in San Juan del Sur, with more than five hundred passengers who came ashore and spent time in nearby Granada and other towns. Many more cruise ships are expected as tourists are no longer kept away by Nicaragua's reputation as a war-torn nation.

In the Workshop

Many Nicaraguans use their skills or crafts in small workshops called *talleres*. Typical jobs in these *talleres* might be making mattresses, tinsmithing, baking, shoemaking, sewing or altering clothes, or doing laundry. Many of these workers are self-employed. Their earnings depend on the amount of work they take in and turn out each week. Generally, the income for these jobs is very low. Families of men who work in the *talleres* usually have other sources of income. For example, a tinsmith's wife might earn money by making and selling tortillas, while their children earn money selling cigarettes on the street.

Nicaragua does not, however, have the obvious attractions of Guatemala and Honduras with their Mayan ruins, nor of Costa Rica which has a well-developed ecotourism industry. But Nicaragua is a country where tourists can enjoy exciting volcanoes, lakes, mountains; unspoiled Pacific

Tourists enjoy a ride on a horse-drawn cart.

beaches; historic colonial cities; and the Caribbean wonder of the Atlantic coast and the Corn Islands. Above all, it has pristine rain forests and an abundance of wildlife essential for the development of ecotourism.

Tourism needs good hotels. Probably Nicaragua's best known world-class resort is Montelimar. A beach house that once belonged to the Somozas has become part of a hotel complex with private beach, four swimming pools, a small zoo, and a casino. The government has offered tax advantages to people ready to invest in Nicaragua's tourism. A start has been made with the building of more hotels in Managua. There are now more tour operators and ecotourism is high on the agenda.

The Pan American Highway

The Pan American Highway is a major transportation route that runs from the Mexico-U.S. border to Puerto Montt, Chile. With the exception of a break through the Darien Gap in Panama, this highway connects the capitals of several countries and covers 29,525 miles (47,516 km). In Nicaragua, a 255-mile (410-km) stretch of the highway runs through the cities of Chinandega, León, Managua, and Rivas. For many years, this highway has been the main road in Nicaragua.

Getting Around

Nicaragua also needs to improve and modernize its transport system, especially for ecotourism, which would focus on forests and swamps in the Atlantic lowlands. The west of the country is reasonably well served, with the Pan American Highway running north to south, though many side roads are not paved and horses and carts are still commonly used.

A bus driver fills a hole in the road while his passengers wait.

There is no good east-west road connection across the country. The journey to Bluefields on the Atlantic coast from Managua is about ten hours by road and river. From Managua to Puerto Cabezas, the road is unpaved and passable only during the dry season from December to April. Air travel is the best alternative and there are daily flights between most of the towns.

After the Storm

In 1998, Arnoldo Alemán's government signed another agreement with the international banks. The government was to continue its program of spending and privatizing industry.

Provided Nicaragua stuck to these policies, it could expect help with the huge sums of money it owed to foreign banks and organizations. Four years earlier, the debt was a staggering US$11 billion, or about US$3,000 for every man, woman, and child in the country at a time when the average pay for workers was less than US$500 for each person. The sum was reduced to about $6 billion in 1998 after international banks and governments agreed to help, but even then it was almost impossible for Nicaragua to meet the interest repayments.

Within months of the agreement, Nicaragua was devastated by Hurricane Mitch. Winds and floods washed away villages, roads, and bridges. It destroyed the coffee harvest and wiped out most other crops. The damage was immense and the Central Bank estimated that total reconstruction costs would be about US$1.5 billion. Recognizing Nicaragua's plight, several countries—including the United States—reduced or wrote off Nicaragua's debt. President Alemán, while recognizing that his country "was on its knees" following the hurricane, nonetheless predicted a rapid recovery.

Slow Going

Many roads in Nicaragua are in need of repair. Even the 40-mile (64-km) journey from Managua to the major resort of Montelimar takes almost two hours. Some roads are built of brick because the Somozas had a brick factory—after the 1972 earthquake President Anastasio Somoza insisted that roads should be reconstructed in brick.

At the Market

What do common supermarket items cost in Nicaragua?

Item	Cost in córdobas (C$)	U.S. equivalent
1 lb rice	C$4	$.33
1 lb beans	C$8	$.66
1 liter oil	C$10	$.78
Toothpaste	C$12	$.98
Coffee, small cup	C$1.5	$.12
1 lb sugar	C$3	$.24
Soft drink	C$5	$.39

The per person income in Nicaragua is equivalent to US$438 per year.

Nicaraguans

Street scene in Managua

N ICARAGUA HAS A POPULATION OF ABOUT 5 MILLION people. They refer to themselves as Nicas. Most Nicas are *mestizos*, people of Spanish and Indian ancestry. Others are descended from Europeans or black Africans. Today, only about 5 percent are Indians.

A high percentage of Nicas are young. In 1998, 44 percent of the population was under fifteen years old, and only 2.6 percent were over sixty-five. Life expectancy is low by international standards, 65 years for men and 69 for women.

Opposite: **Child near Matagalpa**

What's in a Name?

In Nicaragua, many people follow the Spanish custom and have two surnames, or last names. These two names combine the surnames of the mother and father. For example, a girl might be named Juanita Sanchez Rosario. In this case, Sanchez is the father's last name, and Rosario is the mother's family name. If Juanita marries a man called Miguel Benavides Lopez, she will be known as Juanita Sanchez de Lopez.

A young mestizo woman

Population in Major Cities

Managua	1,295,000
León	153,200
Chinandega	120,400
Masaya	110,000
Granada	88,800

Most people live on the plains on the Pacific side of the country, and some 63 percent live in the cities and towns. The people in the western part of the country are largely mestizo and white, though there are a few Indian communities near Léon and in the central highlands. However, there is little to distinguish these small groups from their neighbors, and they have long since lost their native languages.

Nicas live, dress, and work in much the same way as people in North American or Europe, though the majority are of course very much poorer. They do not let this affect their naturally outgoing and generous manner. What little they have, they are always ready to share it with friends and visitors.

Population in Nicaragua

Mestizo	69%
White	17%
Black	9%
Amerindian	5%

Costeños

Less than 10 percent of the population live in the vast forested Atlantic region, which covers about half the country. Here too the majority are mestizos, but this region is also home to Nicaragua's ethnic minorities including the three Indian groups—the Miskito, the Mayagna, and the Rama. Other minorities are the Creoles of African and Spanish descent; and Garifunas, or black Caribs, who have a mixed Indian and African ancestry. They like to be known as *costeños* or "people of the coast."

Costeños have a Caribbean way of life, which is quite different from the peoples of the Pacific side of Nicaragua. English was for a long time the main language and Protestantism rather than Catholicism, the principal religion. Contact between the two sides of Nicaragua is still limited.

The Indians

The Miskito are by far the largest Indian group. They number between 70,000 and 100,000. In the seventeenth and eighteenth centuries, the British equipped the Miskito with guns. These guns were probably muskets, which some people believe gave them the name. They used the guns to capture and trade other Indians as slaves. This largely explains the small number of other Indians.

A Miskito man making a fishing net

By 1850, the Miskito occupied the length of the Atlantic coast from Honduras to Panama. Today, they live in the northeast along the River Coco and close to the border between Nicaragua and Honduras. The border separates them from other Miskito communities in Honduras. Many villages, where the houses were made of mud or thatch, were wiped out by Hurricane Mitch. For those communities in remote and isolated parts of the forest, rescue was particularly difficult.

The Mayagna number about 8,000 and live inland from Puerto Cabezas, the only sizable town on the north Atlantic coast. Sometimes the Mayagna are known as the Sumo, but they regard this as a derogatory name because in their language it means "cowardly." The Rama, who live on Rama Cay, a small island in the Bay of Bluefields, and in Monkey Point, a village south of Bluefields, are a tiny community of perhaps 1,000 people.

The indigenous groups live simply, in the forest, by lakes, or rivers, cultivating crops and fishing. They make handicrafts such as wood carvings, items from bark, and wall hangings. Some indigenous languages have survived. In recent times, these people have found occasional work on banana plantations or with the lumber trade. But there have been many interruptions to disturb their traditional way of life—first, the British and the Spanish; then, the North Americans and others who set up commercial mining, timber, and fruit companies. The Miskito were caught up in the Contra-Sandinista conflict because they lived so close to the Honduran border where the Contras were based.

The 1987 Constitution gave the *costeños* self-rule and divided the Pacific coastal area into the two autonomous regions of RAAN and RAAS. The people formed their own political party and each region elected its own government. Because they have so little experience in modern politics, there have been problems.

A serious dispute arose when the central government granted a logging concession in their region to a foreign company. People in a vast area in northeast RAAN were driven from their land, and a large road was built through the forest. Eventually, the company had to withdraw because of financial problems. Today, the costeños continue to be threatened by lumber and mining companies. Many would now prefer their region to be fully independent from the rest of Nicaragua.

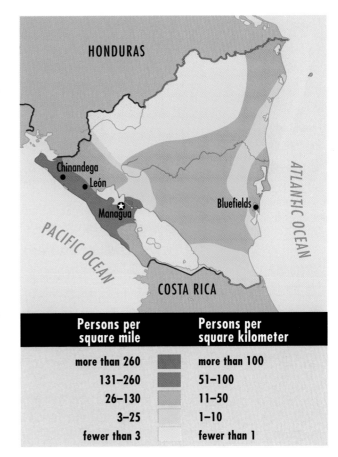

Persons per square mile		Persons per square kilometer
more than 260		more than 100
131–260		51–100
26–130		11–50
3–25		1–10
fewer than 3		fewer than 1

A Creole mother
prepares food.

Creoles are the descendants of European settlers and black Africans brought to work as slaves on the coastal plantations. About 30,000 Creoles make up about 23 percent of the coastal population. They live in and around the main towns of Puerto Cabezas and Bluefields, in Pearl Lagoon, and on the Corn Islands. Many take on menial jobs or work as unskilled labor. However, others have qualified for government and professional employment.

The number of Garifunas in Nicaragua is small, between two and three thousand people. Their background dates from colonial days when black African slaves escaped to the West Indian island of St. Vincent and mixed with the local Carib people. Expelled from St. Vincent, they made their way to islands off the Honduran coast, and then to the mainland. Today, Nicaraguan Garifunas live alongside the Creoles, mainly in Bluefields and the Pearl Lagoon area. They speak English rather than the Garifuna language used by much larger Garifuna communities in Belize and Honduras.

Black people have brought to the Atlantic coast the food, music, and jollity of the West Indies. Bluefields comes alive especially during May, when on weekends the festival of the Maypole takes place. Mostly, the region has the typically relaxed, laid-back atmosphere of the tropics. It is a poor area, there is not much work, and getting around in many places is possible only by river and generally takes many hours. But the people are warm and friendly—despite the incessant rain.

Maypole festival in Bluefields

Women workers at
a tobacco barn

A Woman's Role

Nicaragua has a male-dominated society. As in many Latin
countries, machismo has ensured that women have a sec-

Language

Spanish is the official language of Nicaragua. It is less formal than the Spanish of other parts of Latin America, with elements of Indian languages and a tendency to drop "s" and other letters at the end of words.

On the Atlantic coast, outside the mestizo areas, most people speak English or Creole—a mix of English Spanish, black Carib, and indigenous languages. The indigenous Miskito language is in widespread use. Some school materials are produced in Wangki, one of the Miskito dialects. The Mayagna also have their own language, which is similar to Miskito, but only a very few people now speak Rama. Most of the Rama speak Creole.

The Miskito have incorporated both English and Creole words and adapted them into their language.

The following is a list of numbers one to ten in Miskito and in Miskito/English:

Miskito	Miskito/English	
kum	wan	one
wal	tu	two
yumhpa	tri	three
walhwal	pur	four
matsip	paip	five
matlalkahbi	siks	six
matlalkahbi pura kum	sebm	seven
matlalkabhi pura wal	et	eight
matlalkabhi yumhpa	nain	nine
matawalsip	ten	ten

Women Power

Three out of ten Sandinista soldiers were women. They had an active role, fighting alongside men, carrying combat gear, including rifles. Some women became guerrilla leaders. When the Sandinistas were in government, Dora María Tellez became minister of health and Doris Tijerino was head of the police (she was almost certainly the only woman in the world in such a position). Violeta Chamorro was the first woman president in Central America.

ondary role. Being macho often makes men aggressive and abusive, and a high percentage of Nicaraguan women suffer physically and psychologically at the hands of their husbands. Many women accept this as a normal way of life, but attitudes have been changing since women became involved with the Sandinista revolution and its declared intention of creating equality of the sexes. The revolution also introduced many women for the first time to education and literacy, and different aspects of health and hygiene.

Yet today there are few women in Nicaragua's Congress. The feminist movement is lacking women in top political jobs. However, some organizations have been formed to support and represent women's issues, and women are being encouraged to speak out against violence in the home. An innovative idea has been the establishment of women-only police stations where specially trained policewomen can provide professional guidance.

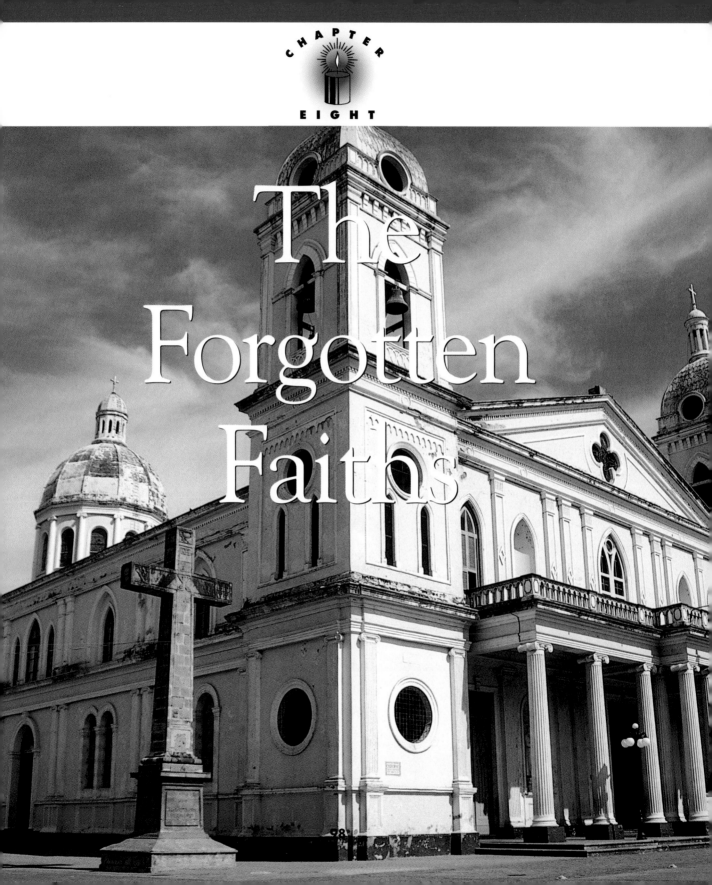

The Forgotten Faiths

WHEN THE FIRST TRAVELERS ARRIVED ON THE CARIBBEAN coast they found the Miskito, Mayagna, and Rama living a simple, self-reliant life. The Miskito respected a father figure or god who lived in the sky, although apparently he was remote and little interested in people. More important were the supernatural beings of the sun, moon, and stars, especially the constellation Pleiades, the seven sisters. All manner of other spirits inhabited natural places such as springs or caves. Contact with the outside world brought changes. Although relics of ancient traditions survive in the memories of older people, the Christian Church came to be widely accepted. However, the power of the Church in Nicaragua has declined in recent years.

Opposite: **Cathedral at Granada**

Interior of the Cathedral Santiago in Managua

At one time, the Catholic clergy had considerable influence in much of the country through its alliance with the ruling classes and landowners. To the east, though, the Atlantic lowlands were another world and largely influenced by the British and other Europeans. Protestant churches became established there in the nineteenth century.

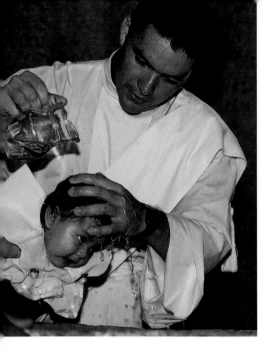

Since 1939 there has been no official state religion in Nicaragua. Although many Nicaraguans may choose a Christian baptism or funeral, their attachment to the Church is minimal. The latter half of the twentieth century saw the involvement of the clergy in political affairs as the movement known as "liberation theology" grew throughout the Latin American region. Liberation theology was a new doctrine that encouraged priests to get involved with their parishioners and help them to create a more just, equal society. Nicaragua's revolution also brought more changes as some of the Catholic clergy took sides with the Sandinistas, while others continued to support wealthy groups.

Baptism in a church in Managua

Ernesto Cardenal

Ernesto Cardenal was born in Granada in 1925. He studied in Mexico and at Columbia University in New York City, and at a Trappist monastery in Gethsemane, Kentucky. He was ordained a priest in 1965.

Opposing the regime of dictator Anastasio Somoza, Cardenal actively supported the Sandinistas. In 1975, Somoza declared Cardenal an outlaw.

Under the new Sandinista government, Cardenal took the position of Minister of Culture, which he held from 1979 until 1988. At present, he is the vice president of Casa de Las Tres Mundos, a cultural organization in Managua.

In addition to being a priest and revolutionary, Cardenal is recognized as an important poet. He is the author of more than thirty-five books in Spanish,

many of which have been translated into English. His books include *Flights of Victory, Zero Hour*, and *The Psalms of Struggle and Liberation*. He considers poetry as a powerful means to bring about change in society and speak out against oppression.

Today, many evangelical churches are working among the Miskito, helping with clinics, education, and faith. In 1999, Baptist missionaries delivered a major shipment of bibles in the Miskito language.

Festival of Purísima

In this country where day-to-day religious life is not obvious, it may seem strange to find crowds drawn to a Catholic saint's

Children participating in Purísima

day procession. Similar festivals in other Latin American countries are attended by pious people, bearing flowers, incense, and religious statues. Nicaraguans love the festival spirit and some remember the meaning behind the tradition. The eighth of December is a public holiday to honour the Immaculate Conception, or Purísima. This feast is observed in many ways—some attend mass in the Catholic churches, others celebrate at home, many just relax. This festival is soon followed by Christmas, which is generally a time for the family to be together and celebrate in the best way their income will allow.

In León there is a special memory attached to the date of the festival. In Spanish colonial days when the

Celebrating Saints' Days

Just about every town and city has its own patron saint, a Roman Catholic saint who is believed to watch over the well-being of the people. Saints' days are celebrated through fiestas, dancing, plays, fireworks, and plenty of music. Here are some cities and their patron saints.

Cities	Saint's Day	Date
Boaco, Managua	Fiesta de Santiago	July 25
Ometepe, Nandaime	Fiesta de Santa Ana	July 26
Managua	Fiesta de Santo Domingo	August 1
Chinandega	Fiesta de San Roque	August 8–16
Masaya	Fiesta de San Miguel	September 29
Pueblo Nuevo	Fiesta de San Rafael	October 29
Catarina	Fiesta de San Silvestre	December 31

church was powerful, the townsfolk once carried a statue of the Blessed Virgin Mary to the foot of the erupting volcano Cerro Negro. According to legend, the volcano became silent and the city was saved.

New Faiths

Modern Nicaragua is receiving more and more attention from evangelical churches and as much as a third of the population are now following a Protestant faith. This phenomenon is not

Cuadros

Families often have small shrines in their homes. These shrines are dedicated to saints who are special to them, sometimes simply because they are related to family birth dates. Pictures of these saints, called *cuadros*, are placed in a position of honor. Candles, flowers, and other decorations surround the cuadro, and prayers are said to enlist the saint's help in everyday matters, such as personal health or finding a new job.

just restricted to Nicaragua. These churches, many funded by religious groups in the United States, have gained ground in much of Latin America.

One reason is certainly the widespread poverty in some areas, especially the cities. People across the region are looking for something to believe in. By providing schools, health facilities, and a welcoming voice, these churches give the people new hope. In Nicaragua new churches are being built and radio broadcasts carry messages of peace and tranquility to the most remote areas. Even in the distant forest of the Bosawas reserve, an evangelical church is helping to educate the Miskito people.

Cultural Traditions

NICARAGUA'S RICH CULTURAL TRADITION DATES BACK to pre-Columbian times. Then people worked with jade and other semiprecious stones, fashioning fine ceramics and ornaments. Today, people in many parts of Nicaragua still make pots decorated with ancient mythological designs, and weave cloth with traditional patterns.

Opposite: **Wire mesh-masks are often worn for festivals.**

A pottery business

This man makes and sells rocking chairs.

People also make hammocks, rocking chairs, baskets, and wicker figures, wood carvings, and leather goods. Pink wire mesh-masks are typically made in Masaya. The masks are generally worn during festivals, but have also been worn by guerrillas in recent wars.

Poetry has dominated the field of literature. Poems by many writers, including Rubén Darío and Ernesto Cardenal are published worldwide. Novels are becoming popular too. Many of the themes reflect the troubles of recent years. Nicaraguan artists and writers have been greatly influenced by the foreign intervention, dictatorship, and revolution that have dominated their country's history. Their creativity, despite the problems and frequent censorship, is quite remarkable.

Rubén Darío

In a land of poets, Rubén Darío stands out as one of the greatest. He is certainly considered "the poet of Nicaragua." Born Felix Rubén García Sarmiento in 1867, Darío led an artistic movement known as *modernismo*, which encouraged writers to break away from traditional forms of poetry. Darío's first major work, *Blue*, was published while he lived in Chile in 1888. *Blue* is a collection of short stories, descriptive sketches, and poetry.

Darío experimented with free verse and explored such subjects as classical mythology, the Orient, Nicaraguan landscapes, and everyday life. In 1896, while working as a diplomat in Buenos Aires, Argentina, he wrote *Profane Hymns and Other Poems*, his second great work.

Darío's greatest work was *Songs of Life and Hope*, published in 1905. The poetry in this volume is an artful mix of tragedy, sorrow, music, and hope. Darío died in 1916.

A monument in Léon honoring Darío shows a woman holding a child.

Giaconda Belli

A New Literature

The poet Rubén Darío led the *modernismo* movement until his death in 1916. The next important literary movement was the *vanguardia*, formed in the 1920s in Granada by writers mostly from elite, conservative backgrounds. Though many of the group initially supported the rebel leader Sandino, most came to support the dictator Somoza Garcia. The group's literary aim was to continue Rubén Darío's work of modernization with an emphasis on all things Nicaraguan. Their poems reflect popular songs, legends and local history, and aspects of their Spanish heritage. One of the group, Pablo Antonio Cuadra, published *Nicaranguan Poems* in 1934. He became one of the country's most revered poets and many of his verses combine ancient Aztec and Mayan mythology, Nicaraguan daily life, and the political mood.

Novelists

Gioconda Belli is both a poet and novelist. She was born in 1948. Belli was thirty years old when she won the prestigious Casa de las Américas poetry prize. Since 1987 she has devoted herself to writing novels. Belli is a strong feminist and her first novel, *The Inhabited Woman*, deals with a woman who rejects her traditional female life to join the armed forces of the revolution. Belli now lives in the United States and in 1996 published *Waslala: Memorial to the Future*. It is a grim portrait of a future in which the environment has been destroyed.

Nicaragua's most distinguished novelist is Sergio Ramirez, the Sandinista vice-president of the early 1990s. Most of his stories concern political events and the life of ordinary people.

Other famous writers include Omar Cabezas. His book *Fire From the Mountain* is a vivid account of his time as a revolutionary fighter. Tomás Borge, one of the founders of the FSLN, won the Casa de las Américas prize for his work *The Patient Impatience*.

Modern Art

Modern art began in Nicaragua in 1948 when Rodrigo Peñalba (1908–1979) became Director of the Escuela Nacional de Bellas Artes (School of Fine Arts). One of his students, Armando Morales, became one of Nicaragua's most acclaimed artists, although he has lived abroad since the 1960s. Among his best-known works are a series of paintings of Augusto Sandino. In the 1960s, some artists formed the Praxis group, of which Alejandro Aróstegui was the leading figure, and they moved Nicaraguan art into a new dimension. They painted abstract art, still life, and landscapes, and used new materials such as sand, glass, and bits of rubbish.

During the 1970s, many artists went abroad to avoid the repression and violence, but the Sandinistas in the 1980s made culture and the arts a priority. Artists had the freedom to express themselves, and received support for new art forms such as muralism. Colorful murals appeared on walls everywhere,

Palacio Nacional de la Cultura

The Palacio Nacional de la Cultura is one of the most historic and interesting buildings in Managua. It is next to the Cathedral de Santiago on the main square and easy to recognize by the fine columns that extend along the front of the building. Nicas know the building well as the Government Palace of the Somoza years. They remember August 22, 1978, when Sandinistas, disguised as National Guard soldiers, stormed the building and seized deputies of the National Assembly.

The Palace has been restored in blue marble and yellow stucco. It is still used for government business, but also houses the Museo Nacional or National Museum.

A mural painted in the naïve style

and one of the most common was a huge portrait of Augusto Sandino in his big hat.

The school of naïve painting became popular. The simple, rural scenes and landscapes painted by Asilia Guillen (1887–1969) were perhaps the best known. During the 1980s, naïve art became a highly successful artistic movement with exhibitions and international recognition. Artists of particular note included Eduardo Arana, Alejandro Guevara, and Marina Silva.

Modern Music

In the west are salsa and son, and in the east, reggae and calypso. Music is part of everyday life in Nicaragua, blaring out from street corners and trucks. Depending on where you are, you will hear music that reflects the country's Spanish, Indian, and African heritage. Guitars and stringed instruments arrived with the Spaniards. Maracas, which are dried-out gourds with seeds that rattle on the inside, date from pre-Columbian times, as do flutes. The most popular instrument

Traditional Music and Dance

Among the few traditions that survived colonial days are music and dancing. Many native people who live in isolated regions of Nicaragua still perform folk dances today. They also play musical instruments that are traced to pre-Columbian times.

Instrument

chirimia	a primitive clarinet
maraca	a rhythm instrument, like a rattle
zul	a flute
quijongo	a one-stringed box-like instrument

Music performed on a street

La Gigantona and *El Gueguense*

La Gigantona or "the giant dancing woman" is often seen in markets, at fiestas, and at political rallies, jigging about to the sound of drums. She is a huge figure, wearing a small crown and long dress. She and Pepe, her tiny sidekick, are entertainers who make fun of politicians and the government. The tradition goes back a long way to the days when Indians mocked the Spaniards.

El Gueguense is a dance-play written centuries ago as a form of protest, though no one knows by whom. The cast, made up of masked figures wearing elaborate costumes, make fun of politicians or protest about issues of the day.

that originated in Africa, the marimba, is similar to a xylophone and carved from a special wood.

Think of revolutionary music in Nicaragua, and you think of the Mejia Godoy brothers, Carlos and Luis Enrique, who were, more than anyone else, responsible for the patriotic songs that accompanied Sandinistas into battle. Carlos wrote the Sandinista anthem, "Nicaragua Nicaraguita" and also composed the very popular "Misa Campesina," a mass for the poor and working classes. Few of the revolutionary songs are heard now, although the "Misa" is still widely performed.

Rock and pop music from North America and Europe are favorites among young people, especially those who party in the many discos in Managua and other cities. Jazz and blues are also played in clubs.

Nicaragua's national sport is baseball, almost certainly introduced by the North American marines early in the twentieth century. Unlike children in most other Latin American countries who enjoy playing soccer, Nicaraguan boys and girls use sticks, tennis balls, or just their arms to play baseball on any empty patch of ground or back yard.

Children playing baseball with homemade ball and bat

Dennis Martinez

On August 9, 1998, Nicaraguan athlete Dennis Martinez broke the record for the most wins by a Latin American pitcher in the United States major leagues. The first Nicaraguan to play in the majors, he began his career with the Baltimore Orioles in 1976. Martinez also played for the Montreal Expos, the Cleveland Indians, and the Seattle Mariners. At thirty-five, he became the oldest player to make an All-Star team for the first time. While with Montreal, in 1991, he pitched a perfect game against the Los Angeles Dodgers. Martinez finished with a 245–193 career record and retired at the age of forty-four, the oldest player in the majors.

Martinez is greatly honored in Nicaragua. In 1998, the government renamed Managua's national stadium in his honor.

Becoming a successful baseball player is a straight route out of poverty. The local hero is Dennis Martinez who played in the major leagues in the United States for twenty-two seasons. Nicaragua has local, regional, and national baseball championships. The national team, known as La Seleccíon, won third place in the world championships in 1998.

Boxing has also provided talented athletes with a way out of poverty. Alexis Arguello, who won three world titles in different weights in the 1970s, was one of nine children. He learned to fight on the streets of Managua. Rosendo Alvarez was also a world boxing champion in the 1990s.

Other popular Nicaraguan sports include soccer, basketball, and volleyball. Little cost is involved and they are popular. On the other hand, tennis, sailing, or golf are for the wealthy few. Traditional spectator sports include bullfighting, which was introduced by the Spaniards, though in Nicaragua the bull is seldom killed. Cockfighting is another spectator sport popular in rural areas, where people place bets on the fighting birds.

Bullfight in Managua

Living and Learning

ORE THAN 60 PERCENT OF NICAS LIVE IN CITIES AND towns. The move from rural areas began in the 1980s when people tried to put a distance between themselves and the war. Their rural homes had been small and primitive—two rooms with a tin roof—but they were often worse off in the cities

Opposite: **A student in Managua**

A dirt road runs past wooden houses.

A barrio in Managua

where there was a shortage of housing. The shanty towns or barrios that mushroomed are very crowded. Usually these areas are a cluster of cardboard, wood, and tin shacks jammed together, often without running water or toilets. Electricity sometimes comes from illegally tapped power lines.

Many Nicaraguans are very poor. Unemployment is high—more than half the people who can work do not have jobs. So they find ways to earn money. This work may include being a street trader who sells all kinds of domestic items— plastic buckets, torches, cigarettes, sweets, cosmetics, clothing, shoes—anything that will fit on a street stall. Women cook food and snacks at home to sell on the streets. Young children look for any kind of small job, such as guarding or cleaning cars.

People survive by working in this way, but they need more than one source of income to afford luxuries. Unfortunately, this need has led to a serious increase in crime.

Children cleaning cars on a Managua street

Compadrazgo

When a Nicaraguan child is baptized, a pair of godparents are named. The godfather is called the *padrino*. The godmother is the *madrina*. Being a godparent is an important responsibility. Godparents are considered co-parents of a child and often assist in taking part in family events. This co-parenting role is called *compadrazgo*, which connects the godparents to the family.

Family Life

Family life has always been very important in Nicaraguan society. Families are quite large, with an average of four children, extended by relatives, godparents, and friends. Often several generations live in one dwelling, and it is common for men and women to live together without being married.

Young men are encouraged to be aggressive from an early age, while young girls are protected. Girls at fifteen are considered ready to enter social life and be prepared for marriage. Families and neighbors depend heavily on each other for help and support and share what they have, including the use of household items such as a refrigerator or a stove.

An extended family

Education for All

Literacy volunteers teach people to read and write.

When the Sandinistas came to power, more than half the population could not read or write. The Sandinistas launched a national literacy crusade. Basic training was given to anyone over the age of twelve who was literate, then these people were sent into the cities and to rural areas to teach others to read and to write. They were helped by volunteers from overseas. About 100,000 *brigadistas*, as they were known, managed within a year to reduce the illiteracy rate from 50 to 13 percent.

National Holidays in Nicaragua

January 1	New Year's Day
May 1	Labor Day
July 19	Liberation Day
September 14	Battle of San Jacinto
September 15	Independence Day
November 2	All Souls' Day
December 8	Immaculate Conception
December 24–26	Christmas

The revolutionary government also built many schools. Cuban teachers were brought in to help. Education was free and compulsory for children at the primary level. Most schools had to run two sessions a day, but it allowed many thousands of children to attend classes for the first time. However, the contras killed and kidnapped many teachers during the war.

After Violeta Chamorro came to power and cut government spending in 1990, there were fewer schools and teachers. Today, about 77 percent of children attend primary school, but only 47 percent make it to the secondary level, which is not free. Many parents cannot afford to pay the small fee or to buy the textbooks.

Private education is available for those who can afford it, and there are four universities. The oldest is the National University founded in 1812, with campuses in Managua and Léon. The newest university is URACCAN, the University of the Autonomous Regions of the Nicaraguan Caribbean Coast. It was founded in 1995, with campuses in Bluefields, Puerto Cabezas, and Siuna.

Health

Nicaragua is not a country of healthy people. Two of the most important requirements for good health are beyond the reach of many Nicaraguans. They do not have enough money to buy nutritional food, and do not have access to clean water.

Opposite: **Schoolchildren on their way to school**

Contaminated water is one of the causes of diarrhea, a major killer of young children. Too often, people have to use the same source of water for drinking, washing clothes, and as a toilet. Other serious diseases caused by polluted water are typhoid and hepatitis. These together with yellow fever, transmitted by mosquitoes, and tuberculosis are still common.

The Sandinista government tackled the country's health problems with more hospitals, doctors, and vaccination programs. Today, about 90 percent of children are immunized against tuberculosis and 80 percent against diphtheria.

For every 100,000 people, Nicaragua has just 82 doctors and 56 nurses. There are not enough hospitals and medical centers and equipment are in short supply. The cost of drugs from a pharmacy is generally more than the average Nicarguan can afford, and many people use traditional remedies of herbs and oils found in most markets.

Getting the News

Several newspapers are published in Nicaragua and most have strong political affiliations. The right-wing press is still firmly rooted in the hands of the Chamorro family who publish *La Prensa*. Other daily newspapers include *El Nuevo Diario*, and the government-owned evening newspaper, *Novedades*. The Sandinista newspaper, *Barricada*, closed in early 1998. None of the papers have a large circulation because people cannot afford to buy them. Instead, in most homes, people rely on radios for their news, and increasingly on a television shared by family and friends. Apart from news, television is most

enjoyed for its soap operas or *telenovelas*, broadcast from other
Latin American countries. North American films and car-
toons are also popular.

Daily Dishes

Typical dishes of Nicaragua's west and east are very different. The nearest to a national dish is *gallo pinto* or "painted rooster." In the west, it is eaten every day in most homes. It comprises the two basic foods of rice and beans, spiced with garlic and onions.

In the east, "run down" is a coconut stew with many ingredients—coconut milk, onions, herbs, banana and plantain, yucca, taro root, dasheen, breadfruit, yam, together with meat or fish. Fish is plentiful on the Atlantic coast. In the highlands and on the west coast, maize tortillas and tamales filled with meat or cheese and wrapped in banana leaves are basic foods. Other, rather more special, meals are *chicharrones* or fried pork skins, and *vigoron* which is boiled cassava topped with *chicharrones* and cabbage salad. *Vabo* or *babo* is a rich soup of beef or pork served with vegetables.

In good years, fruit and vegetables are plentiful in most areas. Fresh drinks are made from fruits such as mango, papaya, and tamarind, as well as *pitahaya*, a bright magenta fruit from a type of cactus. *Pinolillo* is a drink made from toasted corn, cocoa, water, and milk.

Bianca Jagger

Perhaps still best known as the ex-wife of British rock star Mick Jagger, Bianca Jagger has spent much of her time campaigning for human rights. Born in Nicaragua in 1945, Bianca Pérez Morena de Macias Bom studied in Managua and in Paris at the Institute of Political Studies.

Central America was the focus of her attention in the 1980s, when atrocities were being committed in several countries by government troops, death squads, and guerrillas. She was also concerned with environmental issues and was at the forefront of campaigns to save the rain forests in Nicaragua and Brazil. More recently, she has helped highlight the plight of the Yanomani Indians in Brazil, and in exposing human rights violations in the former Yugoslavia.

In recognition of her work, she has received awards from the United Nations and many other organizations. She regularly contributes articles to newspapers and magazines.

The Future

A great deal has happened in the last twenty years in Nicaragua. It is difficult to predict what will happen next. Without doubt, the people of Nicaragua have suffered more than most people with their country devastated by war, the economy on its knees, and its harvests destroyed by hurricanes. Yet Nicaraguans still smile, their warmth and generosity are unmistakable. They hope for a better future but in the meantime are grateful for what they have. As eleven-year-old Jonny Chavarría of Solentiname wrote:

> I am happy because I have my parents
> I am happy because I can read
> I am happy because I am a poet.

Timeline

Nicaraguan History		World History	
		2500 B.C.	Egyptians build the Pyramids and the Sphinx in Giza.
		563 B.C.	The Buddha is born in India.
		A.D. 313	The Roman emperor Constantine recognizes Christianity.
		610	The Prophet Muhammad begins preaching a new religion called Islam.
		1054	The Eastern (Orthodox) and Western (Roman) Churches break apart.
		1066	William the Conqueror defeats the English in the Battle of Hastings.
		1095	Pope Urban II proclaims the First Crusade.
		1215	King John seals the Magna Carta.
		1300s	The Renaissance begins in Italy.
		1347	The Black Death sweeps through Europe.
		1453	Ottoman Turks capture Constantinople, conquering the Byzantine Empire.
		1492	Columbus arrives in North America.
		1500s	The Reformation leads to the birth of Protestantism.
Spanish arrive in today's Nicaragua.	1522		
Nicaragua comes under the rule of the Audiencia of Guatemala.	1570		
English take control of Mosquito Coast.	1600s		
		1776	The Declaration of Independence is signed.
		1789	The French Revolution begins.

Nicaraguan History

Nicaragua declares its independence from Spain.	1821
Nicaragua, Costa Rica, Guatemala, Honduras, and El Salvador form a Central American Federation.	1823
William Walker invades Nicaragua.	1855
British gives up Mosquito Coast to Spain.	1860
Telegraph service begins in Nicaragua.	1876
José Santos Zelaya is overthrown.	1909
Earthquake destroys Managua.	1931
Augusto Sandino is assassinated.	1934
Anastasio Somoza becomes president.	1937
Somoza is assassinated.	1956
The Sandinista National Liberation Front is founded.	1961
Earthquake flattens Managua.	1972
Somoza regime is overthrown; Sandinistas come to power.	1979
Daniel Ortega is elected president of Nicaragua.	1984
U.S. Congress approves aid to Nicaraguan Contras.	1985
Violeta Barrios de Chamorro becomes president.	1990
Arnoldo Alemán is inaugurated as president.	1997

World History

1865	The American Civil War ends.
1914	World War I breaks out.
1917	The Bolshevik Revolution brings communism to Russia.
1929	Worldwide economic depression begins.
1939	World War II begins, following the German invasion of Poland.
1945	World War II ends.
1957	The Vietnam War starts.
1969	Humans land on the moon.
1975	The Vietnam War ends.
1979	Soviet Union invades Afghanistan.
1983	Drought and famine in Africa.
1989	The Berlin Wall is torn down, as communism crumbles in Eastern Europe.
1991	Soviet Union breaks into separate states.
1992	Bill Clinton is elected U.S. president.
2000	George W. Bush is elected U.S. president.

Fast Facts

Official name: Republic of Nicaragua

Capital: Managua

Carriage rolling past a cathedral

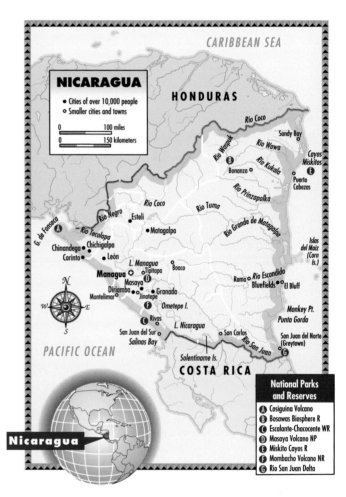

NICARAGUA

- Cities of over 10,000 people
- Smaller cities and towns

0   100 miles
0   150 kilometers

CARIBBEAN SEA

HONDURAS

Rio Coco

Sandy Bay

Rio Wospuk

Rio Wawa

Cayos
Miskitos

Bonanza

Rio Kukala

Puerto
Cabezas

Rio Prinzapolka

Rio Coco

Esteli

Rio Tuma

Matagalpa

Rio Grande de Matagalpa

Islas
del Maiz
(Corn
Is.)

Rio Negro

G. de Fonseca

Rio Tecolapa

Chinandega   Chichigalpa

Corinto   León

L. Managua

Boaco

Rama   Rio Escondido

Bluefields   El Bluff

Managua   Tipitapa

Masaya

Diriamba   Granada

Montelimar   Jinotepe

Ometepe I.

Monkey Pt.
Punta Gorda

Rivas

San Juan del Sur

Salinas Bay

L. Nicaragua

San Carlos

San Juan del Norte
(Greytown)

Rio San Juan

PACIFIC OCEAN

Solentiname Is.

COSTA RICA

Nicaragua

National Parks and Reserves

- A Cosiguina Volcano
- B Bosawas Biosphere R
- C Escalante-Chacocente WR
- D Masaya Volcano NP
- E Miskito Cayos R
- F Mombacho Volcano NR
- G Rio San Juan Delta

Nicaragua's flag

View of Concepción

Official language:	Spanish
Major religion:	Roman Catholic
Founding date:	Independence, 1522
National anthem:	"Nicaragua"
Government:	Republic
Chief of state:	President
Head of government:	President
Area:	49,998 square miles (129,494 sq km)
Highest elevation:	Pico Mogotón, 6,913 feet (2,107 m) above sea level
Lowest elevation:	Sea level along the Pacific Ocean.
Longest river:	Rio Coco, 485 miles (780 km)
Largest lake:	Lake Nicaragua, 3,150 square miles (8,159 sq km)
Greatest annual precipitation:	297 inches (755 cm), at Bluefields
Lowest annual precipitation:	46 inches (117 cm) at Managua
Average annual temperature:	80°F (27°C). There is less than 4°F difference between winter and summer temperatures in Nicaragua.
National population (2000 est.):	4,812,569

Three-toed sloth

Currency

Population of largest cities (2001 est):

Managua	1,295,000
León	153,200
Chinandega	120,400
Masaya	110,000
Granada	88,800

Famous landmarks:
- ▶ *Lake Nicaragua*
- ▶ *National University* in León
- ▶ *Roman Catholic Cathedral* in León
- ▶ *Palacio Nacional de la Cultura* in Managua
- ▶ *Presidential Palace* in Managua
- ▶ *Pico Mogotón*
- ▶ *Corn Islands*
- ▶ *Bosawas Biosphere Preserve*

Industry: Food processing, chemicals, machinery and metal products, textiles, clothing, petroleum refining, beverages, footwear, wood, cotton, coffee, sugarcane, bananas, beef, rice, tobacco, corn, beans, sesame, gold, silver, copper, tungsten, lead, zinc.

Currency: Nicaragua's monetary unit is the gold córdoba (C$). One córdoba equals 100 centavos. US$1 = C$13.3.

Weights and measures: Metric system, except gasoline, which is sold by the gallon.

Literacy rate: 77%

Nicaraguan children

Ernesto Cardenal

Common words and phrases:

¡Hola!	Hello!
Muchas gracias.	Many thanks
¿Hablas tu inglés?	Do you speak English?
No comprendo.	I don't understand.
¿Cómo estás?	How are you?
Tengo hambre.	I'm hungry.
Tengo sed.	I'm thirsty.
Ayúdame. Me he perdido.	Help me. I'm lost.

Famous Nicaraguans:

Ernesto Cardenal (1925–)
Catholic priest, revolutionary, and poet

Violeta Barrios de Chamorro (1929–)
Political leader

Rubén Darío (1867–1916)
Poet and journalist

Bianca Jagger (1945–)
Human-rights activist

Daniel Ortega Saavedra (1945–)
Political leader

Augusto César Sandino (1895–1934)
Political leader

Anastastio Somoza (1896–1956)
Political leader

José Santos Zelaya (1853–1919)
Political leader

To Find Out More

Books

▶ Haverstock, Nathan A. *Nicaragua in Pictures (Visual Geography)*. Minneapolis: Lerner Publishing Group, 1993.

▶ Kott, Jennifer. *Nicaragua* (Cultures of the World). New York: Times Books International, 1995.

▶ Plunkett, Hazel. *Nicaragua in Focus: A Guide to the People, Politics and Culture*. New York: Interlink, 1999.

▶ Stockwell, John. *Daniel Ortega*. Broomall, PA: Chelsea House, 1991.

Websites

▶ **Art and Music of Nicaragua**
http://www.bcn.gob.ni
The official site of Nicaragua's National Bank, in Spanish with a good cultural section including music for downloading and examples of art by Nicaraguan painters.

▶ **U.S. Library of Congress**
http://lcweb2.loc.gov/frd/cs/ nitoc.html
A country profile with numerous links.

Embassies and Organizations

▶ **Embassy of the Republic of Nicaragua**
1627 New Hampshire Avenue, N.W.
Washington, DC 20009
(202) 939-6570
http://www.embassy.org/embassies/
ni.html

Index

Page numbers in *italics* indicate illustrations.

Meet the Author

"**M**Y LIFE HAS BEEN TIED TO LATIN AMERICAN LIFE since I left university." With just a few exceptions that include work in West Africa and Scandinavia, Marion Morrison has devoted her energies to understanding the affairs of Latin America.

"As a student of history, I tend to look first at the way events of the past have shaped what is happening today. Central America is an intensely powerful story which, very sadly, is steeped in conflict. That has left its mark." Marion has not looked back since the days she worked as a volunteer with a flagship UN program in the Andes Mountains. Since then she has traveled widely, often with her documentary film-maker husband. Together they have ventured to some of the most remote parts of the continent and the most populous. "In recent years I have seen cities expanding with shanties growing like mushrooms on ground I first saw as fields. People are everywhere. Nicaragua with so much land and such a small population is quite different."

To keep up-to-date when not traveling, Marion is in constant touch with friends made over the years. "At one time we received several letters a day with stamps through the regular post. Now it's almost all e-mail, but I suppose it's faster. We also have a specialist library of books and regularly attend lectures and concerts in London devoted to Latin American life."

Photo Credits

Photographs © 2002:

AP/Wide World Photos/Erik S. Lesser: 114

Corbis Sygma: 63 (Bleibtreu), 100 bottom, 133 bottom (Giannini), 68, 75, 82, 115 (Diego Goldberg), 11 (La Prensa-Nicaragua)

Corbis-Bettmann/Reuters NewMedia Inc.: 20

Cory Langley: 26, 66, 78, 79, 85, 98, 99, 110 top, 132 bottom

Dr. Jaime Incer: 15, 17, 23, 28, 29, 30, 31, 33, 34, 39 bottom, 41, 44, 46 top, 46 bottom, 50, 95

Impact Visuals: 80, 121 (Larry Boyd), 96 (Olivia Heussler), 60, 72 (Jeff Perkell), 118 (Cindy Reiman), 127 (Rick Reinhard), cover, 6 (Sean Sprague)

Instituto de Historia de Nicaragua y Centroamerica, Universidad Centroamerica, Managua: 49, 51 bottom, 52 right, 52 left, 53, 54, 55 bottom, 55 top, 57, 58, 59, 64, 65, 107, 108 bottom

MapQuest.com, Inc.: 67

Oscar C. Williams: 111

Panos Pictures: 74, 81 (Tina Gue), 116 (Betty Press), 27 (Paul Smith), 9, 14 top, 84, 88, 89, 100 top, 110 bottom (Jon Spaull), 76, 101, 112 (Sean Sprague)

Photo Researchers, NY: 35 (Geoff Bryant), 43 (Renee Lynn), 42 (Martin Wendler/Okapia), 32 (Jeanne White), 36, 132 top (Art Wolfe)

South American Pictures: 1, 12, 24, 106, 123, 133 top (Robert Francis), 7 top, 7 bottom, 13, 22, 25, 45, 73 top, 86, 90, 94, 103, 104, 108 top 117, 119, 126, 131 top (Jason P. Howe), 83 top (Elin Hoyland), 14 bottom, 37, 38, 39 top, 77 (Tony Morrison)

The Image Works: 19, 61 (L. Dematteis), 18 (A. Farnsworth), 92 (Debbie Hird), 113, 120 (R. Kalman)

Woodfin Camp & Associates: 8, 105, 125, 130 left (Betty Press), 97 (Olivier Rebbot)

Maps by Joe LeMonnier.